# More Dimes From Heaven

# More Dimes From Heaven

## A Journey to Self-Publishing

Monica L. Morrissey

Chelsea Collier

Monica L. Morrissey LLC

## Dedication

To both of my parents, James and Deanna Palmer.
I know you are always with me now. Thank you for your
guidance during this lifetime.

# Acknowledgments

Thank you to my husband, Brian, who always encourages me to follow my dreams. Thank you to my Father-in-law and Mother-in-law, who taught me to have gratitude for everything in life.

Thank you to my two sons, Shamus and Patrick, for being who you are. I hope you always enjoy life to the fullest with Emily and Heather!

Thank you to my darling Grandsons, Lincoln James Morrissey and Jackson Douglas Morrissey. I love spending time with you both!

Thank you to my Sister, Debbie, for always being there for me.

Thank you to Merrilee and Don, who treat me like their daughter.

Thank you to my team- Chelsea and Tracy Collier. You both cheer me on and support me in ways that thank you just doesn't seem enough. I cherish our time together and so appreciate having you with me in this journey of life!

Thank you to my Editor in chief, Kim Knudson. Thank you for your support and your knowledge of the English Language.

In my first book, I wrote about building walls up to protect myself. I built a wall with my boss when I was 19 years old but am thankful that Barb Grant is back in my life now. I so appreciate our friendship and great conversations. Thank you for your advice on my book and in life!

Thank you to all of my Readers- I love to hear your stories about signs from your loved ones. Thank you for your continued support and I hope you enjoy Book #2!

# A Note From the Author

*Dimes from Heaven, How Coins and Coincidences Helped Me Discover My Life as an Empath* came from my soul. It was a journey within myself that I hadn't planned to do. It was as much of a surprise to me as it was to many of my friends and family. I was honored that people enjoyed reading my story.

*More Dimes from Heaven, A Journey to Self* Publishing is a bit different that my first book. The one thing that is the same is that there are many dimes within the story. There are also other messages from my Angels in Heaven that were sent during my writing journey. The reader hears these stories along with some other topics to think about. Each chapter has questions to help you write your story or book. The last part of each chapter is my experience and knowledge about how to self-publish. I hope to encourage you to share your story with the world!

Connect with me:
Facebook @monicalmorrissey
Facebook group https://www.facebook.com/groups/dimesfromheaven
Website www.monicalmorrissey.com
Email monicalmorrissey@gmail.com

# Table of Contents

# More Dimes From Heaven, A Journey to Self Publishing

## Introduction- From Teacher to Author: Following My Soul's Journey

**"The Secret is the law of attraction! Everything that's coming into your life you are attracting into your life. And it's attracted to you by virtue of the images you're holding in your mind. It's what you're thinking. Whatever is going on in your mind you are attracting to you." ~ Rhonda Byrne**

On the night of my first book signing event, I saw a young woman, a friend of my son, and I shared with Renae that I was having my first book signing. The name of the event was Messages From Heaven, where the same Medium, Rebecca Anne LoCicero (https://www.rebeccaannelocicero.com/) that I wrote about in my first book would be doing a group event. I shared with her the story when the Medium said, "A dime a dozen." Sitting in the front row, I held up my dime necklace and Rebecca said, "*Is that a F\*@king dime?*". My father came through with a lot of messages for me. The dimes were my Dad's way to communicate because he had given me a special dime from his coin collection. Renae responded, "*You are so lucky!*" I would love to say that it is luck. I responded, "*It might be luck but it is because I am so open. I used to close down my heart because I was scared to be hurt. Now, I am open so these things tend to happen more often!*" She agreed and I walked away hoping that her heart would be a little more open because she felt it was safe. I also hoped that Renae would get messages from her Dad.

**"What some people call luck and coincidence is the precise execution of an infinitely intelligent universe that works in amazing ways to fulfill exactly what we imagine ourselves to be, with conviction." ~ David Cameron Gikandi**

My husband and I are back at the condo in Indian Shores, Florida, exactly one year after I began writing *Dimes from Heaven*. I get asked the question, "How long did it take you to write your book?" I began writing in early April of 2018 on our annual spring vacation in Florida, sent my manuscript to the publisher (I self-published through Balboa Press, a division of Hay House)on January 8th, 2019 and my book was released on February 27, 2019. It took me approximately nine months. I don't think this is the average, especially if you have a traditional publisher. My book seemed to literally appear out of nowhere from the beginning to the end, an unexpected blessing in my life.

Originally, I set out to write my dime story- nothing more than a neat short story. I started writing because I was in physical pain and the doctors couldn't figure out why my bladder felt like I had to urinate all the time. It was awful and I had gone from doctor to doctor with no relief. Somewhere along my travels I had heard that writing was therapeutic. I seriously rolled my eyes as I put pen to paper. *How would writing heal a physical pain? This was crazy! When I had physical pain, wasn't I supposed to go to the doctors? They would give me something that could heal me. If I had to look at my emotions to heal, how long would that take? Plus, that sounded way too difficult and time consuming!*

I kept writing because I wanted to share my dime story. I envisioned myself making photocopies for friends and family - imagining it would be like 10 pages total. Then, when I first started writing, my husband asked me if I was writing a book. I never thought I would have enough of a story to make it into a book. He had planted a seed that grew into an idea. Then that idea turned into a reality. Never in my entire 50 years had I EVER wanted to write a book!

Writing was for "other" people! As a teacher, I enjoyed teaching Math and actually hated to teach writing. I wanted my students to enjoy the creative free writing but the curriculum wanted me to direct them in not only how to write but also what to write about. I wanted them to write about whatever they were interested in. You have ducks for a pet? Tell me a story about your ducks! You have a horse? Tell me about your horse. You have a cool grandpa? Write about your favorite day with him. Write about whatever you feel in your heart.

That's how you, too, can find out what you want to write about. Your husband had a stroke? Write about your story to help the next person who might be going through the same thing. You have cancer? Write about it to help the next person who has cancer. You adopted a child? Share your story - all of it - the good, the bad, and yes, the ugly. Be authentically *you* in every way. Be brave because not only is it possible that you help the next person in your shoes, you can also help yourself.

I was scared to share a lot of my story, but I also knew that I needed to share. I had faith that it would help someone, somewhere and it most definitely did!

In *Dimes from Heaven*, when my husband and I were chatting about my writing, he said that the wire cable near the pool area was there all along, even though I couldn't see it. The sun blinded me from being able to see the cable.

*"Has my ability to write and listen to my intuition been within me all this time? Were the answers inside me all the time, but I wasn't looking the right way to be able to see them?" ~Monica L. Morrissey*

*I hadn't been able to see that I could listen to my intuition and write a book. I thought maybe my ability to write had been there all along but I hadn't been able to see it because I wasn't looking at it the right way; I was too busy being angry and feeling resentment.*

*This year, we swim in the pool and I say, "There's that wire, but there isn't one on this side of the pool. You know- the one I saw last year?" He responds, "You have to be on the other side to see it. It's there." His words have a deeper meaning for me. I think of being on the other side of publishing my book. I am a different person now. I can't quite explain it but something in me has shifted.*

**"The unknown carries tremendous opportunities, knowledge, potential, and rewards. Step into it often." ~ David Cameron Gikandi**

It all feels like a dream. Last year, on our way to the airport, I stopped at Barnes and Noble. I found a beautiful turquoise journal and wrote on the front cover, "More Than a Dime." My 'dime story' was so much more, but, even then, I had no road map as to where I was going with my writing. I listened to the voice inside; it was time to share my story.

I started writing the day we got to Florida. Once I started, I didn't want to stop. I was dumping a lot of emotional baggage onto the pages. In between those stories, the dime story began to appear. It would be transformed over the next several months, but the 'bones' of the story would be developed that first week.

It was like a secret portal connected to a universal intelligence opened up for me. One that I had not dared to go through for fear of someone not liking me. I was scared to be me. I was scared to share my story. When I allowed myself to be me and be present (at this point I was just learning mindfulness practices), the portal opened up even more and I was able to see the universe in a whole, new way. God, my Angels, and my Spirit Guides were all there ready to support me. They were there because I asked for their help. I spoke the words out loud instead of just thinking about them in my head. I felt the connection inside my body. That's the only way to open up the secret "portal" I began experiencing.

The portal opened up because I was feeling and not just thinking. The mindfulness training had brought me back into my body instead of always being in my head. I was paying attention to my thoughts and the sensations within myself. The portal connecting me to the universe was guiding me in a new direction and I was stepping into something that I felt was unplanned. This new access to the portal was the beginning of my spiritual awakening.

**"You always have the choice to *pay attention* and take an unfamiliar and perhaps risky path. Likewise, you can choose to *not pay attention* and stay with the version of your life implanted in you by familial and cultural influences dictating precisely what your limitations and aspirations ought to be." ~ Dr. Wayne Dyer**

Writing is a journey that opened my eyes to a whole other world; one I knew little about. It was a world I was, at first, scared to enter. I had to have faith that it was a work I was destined to be a part of. I was stepping into the unknown with a knowing that I was exactly where I was supposed to be at the exact time I was meant to be there.

I never once in my life thought I would actually write a book. Within the first two weeks of receiving feedback from my readers, one reader (whom I did not know) wrote an Amazon Review, *"To pour your heart out and tell your story was amazing to read. It is nice to know that I can relate to some of the stories. If you are looking for your next book, please consider this book. I had a hard time to put it down, once I started reading it. **Thank You for sharing and I look forward to reading more, if you continue to share."*** I looked at my husband and said, "Oh my goodness. I'm not ready for that! I don't know what I would write about!" He responded, in his usual supportive manner, *"You'll figure it out."*

Just like I hadn't thought of taking a different path when there was a rock blocking my path, I had absolutely no idea what to do next. I hadn't prepared myself for this. *Was there really any way to truly prepare for a book release?* For me, it was a wait and see what happens. I didn't know what to expect and now the readers wanted more!

I began to observe my life - like I was watching from the outside looking in. *What was happening? I listened to my readers. What were they asking about?* A lot of them seemed interested in writing their own story. My story gave them the courage to want to share their story. They asked questions like, *"Why did you write your book?"* or *"How did you get your book published?"* When I listen to the universe, it seems to have the answer I was seeking. I would write a book about my writing journey- which, in and of itself, was pretty spectacular!

In *Dimes from Heaven*, the readers heard my thoughts of how scared I was to write and tell my story to the world. What the readers didn't hear about were all the crazy signs from the universe when I started writing. Unbelievable things happened to show me I was taking a whole new path in life and everything was going to be ok. I listened to my own advise and believed that I was following my soul's journey in a whole new exciting way.

I kept track of all the mysterious synchronicities that were happening. Originally they were all included in the manuscript. They were cut when my publisher told me the cost of the book would be $58.99! *What? That's CRAZY! That price was way too high!* When I self-published, I didn't get a say in setting the book price. Even without this section, the price of the book was going to be $32.99. By cutting that part out, I realized that there was a reason for it. I would be able to share my story about becoming an author to help the next person write their story! I thought it was unplanned, but I think the universe had planned this.

Brené Brown states that the opposite of belonging is fitting in. I think what she means is that if I am fitting in, then I am trying to be like everyone else. But, if I truly belong, then others accept me as I am and I can be me without having to change to fit in.

**I have spent most of my life trying to fit in. I have tried to be like other people instead of me.** You are reading this today because my readers were willing to see me as my true self and did not ask me to "fit in". I first had to see myself and then allow you to see me.

I have been hiding for 50 years. **I have been within myself searching for a sense of belonging. What I didn't understand was that in order to belong, I had to accept myself first and the rest would happen automatically.** I had to understand that we all belong to the universe. We are all connected to something greater than ourselves. We are all exactly who we are supposed to be. *What does belonging mean to you now that you know to seek it through loving yourself versus fitting in?*

**"The real benefit of looking back at all of those significant events of your life and seeing how that invisible hand of God was there for you at the time is not to rehash your entire past looking for the hidden meanings, but to awaken you to becoming a more conscious person now, today, in the present moments of your life." ~ Dr. Wayne Dyer**

My Dad loved to have conversations about a bigger purpose in life. We had many conversations about coincidences or synchronicities when I was caring for him after my Mom transitioned to Spirit. I knew that he missed her a lot but we tried to feel connected to her through signs that we felt were from Heaven. Once my Dad transitioned to Spirit, I knew that he had figured out the Spirit Communication System I had told him about.

**"Hey dad- there is this new communication system you haven't heard of yet. It's a new Spirit Communication system. It's where angels in Heaven can talk to humans on earth. It's awesome and works well. You won't really be away from us. We will be able to talk all the time. I can talk to you and you can talk to me. We will always know that you are here with us. It's kind of like a new telephone system (my dad was a mechanic and always had to understand the details of how things worked). It works so well you will be able to call me anytime and I can call you too! Mom has already tried the new system and she is excited for you to join her. Your Mom is there too! Your Mom is waiting for you. You can send messages anytime you want and we will all talk to you too." ~Monica L. Morrissey**

My Dad had given me a special dime from his coin collection. It was called a Liberty Head Dime or a Mercury Dime. It symbolized Freedom of Thought and he had it made into a necklace for all of his children and grandchildren. Since my mother had passed away, she had been sending me pennies from Heaven. I knew when I started receiving dimes, they were my dad communicating with me.

There are more dime stories in this book, but they are sprinkled throughout my story. It isn't like the last book where you knew some of the dimes would be at the end. This time, you are going to be reading and then all of a sudden - there is a dime story! That is what life is like with unexpected surprises all along the way.

**Note from the author:** Each chapter is set up to encourage you to dig deep to uncover your story. You might journal along and answer the questions I propose or you might even write your own book! I hope you enjoy the stories along my journey to becoming an author.

"**By taking the courageous step of sharing a story that is deeply true to you, that makes you feel vulnerable and has real emotion, you will experience a new feeling of personal power, and your audience will feel that power too.**" ~ Heather Box and Julian Mocine-McQueen

-

1

## Chapter One:  My Career Path

**"When you are working within your purpose, work is no longer a job; it becomes a pleasure, and it becomes life. The boundary between work and fun vanish." David Cameron Gikandi**

I graduated High School in 1986 and went to college to become a teacher. At this point in time, most guidance counselors were encouraging students to attend college. The question wasn't, "What are you passionate about?" but more like, "What career path will provide you a safe, secure life?" I thought everyone was going to college so that's what I did too. It wasn't, "Should I go to college?" It was, "Where do I go to college?" After I figured out where to go, "What do I want to study to provide me with money?"

I applied and was accepted into two colleges - Johnson State College (ten minutes away from my childhood home) or The University of Vermont (about an hour away). I felt Johnson was a better fit for me; both financially and socially. Since my parents didn't allow me much freedom in high school, I couldn't imagine going to Burlington - which seemed like a big city to me at the time!

I had two career paths I was interested in. I loved working with numbers but I also loved babysitting children. I either wanted to be a Certified Public Accountant or a teacher.  My mother went to Johnson

State College in the 1950's to receive her Elementary Education teaching license. She only taught for a very short time before becoming a stay at home Mom and helping my Dad with the family business. Johnson State was known for their education program so that also contributed to my decision about where I decided to go to college.

If you read *Dimes from Heaven*, then you know my first year in college was pretty tough. I had no idea how to make friends and I was so insecure that I turned to alcohol for confidence. After that first year, I met my husband and was able to get more focused on studying.

Because I was young in my class, I graduated college at age 21 and began my first year teaching. It was 1990. I graduated college in May, got married in August and began teaching 6th grade in the fall. It was a whirlwind of a year and I grew up fast. I had a big class that year and I did not feel very confident in my teaching. I had no mentor to guide me and felt like I was thrown into a sink or swim situation.

I remember that year. My students and parents were a great group. I felt very supported by the families, my colleagues and the principal. I was making a few mistakes here and there, but everyone was very supportive. On the other hand, because I internalized all of my stress, I ended up getting very sick with shingles that year. Looking back now, I would imagine that if I had practiced self care as I do now I might have avoided this illness.

I loved my job as a teacher and at one point, I thought, "Wow. They are actually paying me to do the very thing that I love to do! How amazing is that?" I was having so much fun with my students and watching them grow that I sometimes forgot that this was a job.

**"The surest way to enjoy your work is to work within your purpose in life. Work within whatever you determine is your purpose in life, not your job or obligation, but that which you feel called from within to do, that which you dream of doing- and joy at work will be easy to experience." ~ David Cameron Gikandi**

The years as a teacher seemed to literally fly by. I was a busy working Mom of two boys. I worked as a teacher taking care of everyone else and then came home to take care of my family. Teaching offered me a lot of time to spend with my boys. We loved to spend time doing fun things outside, especially camping and going to the beach in the summer.

When my boys were teenagers and got their licenses, I had more free time for me. I don't do well with time on my hands; I like to be busy. I decided that I would work part-time as a Realtor. At the time, we were trying to sell our house and I thought it might be an interesting job.

Originally, I began working as a Realtor for extra money. The extra income would help our family be able to go on a vacation and help our boys with the insurance and vehicle costs of being a new driver. It took me some time to realize that for me, Real Estate isn't just about the money. It's about helping people. Buying a new home is a big decision. I had to reframe my thinking about Real Estate from a "I want this deal to go through for the money" to "I want to help people find their perfect home". I had to understand that the universe had a bigger purpose for me.

*"Was being a realtor supposed to teach me to believe in letting the future unfold instead of trying to control it? Was it forcing me to feel out of control so that I could learn ultimately that God is in control?...I had to learn to let go of the outcome." ~Monica L. Morrissey*

I can see clearly that the knowledge of how the real estate market worked was extremely useful information to have when I helped my parents sell their long time family business and when we sold their houses as part of their estate. I never could have known at the time, but the universe was giving me an opportunity to prepare myself for the events that would come later.

I promised myself when I was young that I would never be a grumpy, angry teacher. I started to become that person and knew that I had to do something different. I loved teaching but I was taking on everyone's energy (and didn't understand it at the time!). I was turning into the angry person I didn't want to be. I sometimes showed this side of myself in the classroom, but tried hard not to. Often times, I would react to things that happened to me at school in a very defensive way. Parent complaint? *Well, let me tell you what I think about them!* Administration problem? *Well, I can tell you what they should be doing.* I was becoming a defensive "know it all" anytime I felt threatened or attacked. Small things could send me into a tailspin of stories that would ultimately make me out to be the victim of injustices done to me. I didn't understand that this is how we are built as humans, but I knew that I had to do something different with my life.

While writing, I learned that I was an empath. This affected my teaching career and eventually, because I did not take care of myself, it caused me to be sick. As an empath and highly sensitive person, I physically and emotionally absorb other people's energy. This is wonderful if I am near a positive person, but with so much negativity in the world today, I was taking on too much negative energy. I also thought it was my job to fix everything. This was too much for me and I eventually got burned out being around people so much. Teaching was becoming a career that I couldn't do anymore because it was impossible to take care of myself and everyone else. My nervous system was overloaded and I had no strategies of how to care for myself.

I worked toward my Master's degree and thought I might want to be a Principal. When I was about to graduate, I interviewed and was a finalist for three Principal positions. I remember getting the phone call that I didn't get the job. I was runner up. I called my husband and I said, "I'm ok with not getting the job. I am upset because I know that I can't keep teaching. I HAVE to do something else with my life." I had no idea that the universe had a plan and I needed to be patient.

Weeks later, I got the perfect job. It wasn't a job as a Principal. The universe knew, even before I knew, that being a principal would be too physically and emotionally demanding for me. I needed a job where I would be able to take better care of myself. In this new job as a Curriculum Director, I would begin to love helping teachers, which in turn helped students. While doing this, I would be able to balance my work and home life better. I would slowly learn that I was more than my job.

**"I was pushing, striving, and controlling, instead of listening, trusting, and allowing. It took my whole life to come tumbling down for me to realize that everything I was searching for was inside me all along."** ~ Rebecca Campbell

In my book *Dimes from Heaven*, there is a chapter called **Come What May.** I tell the story of when I had bought a ring with this saying on it and at the time, I place the words facing toward me so that I was able to read the words. Recently, I started wearing the ring again. This time, though, I placed the words facing the other direction. It might seem like an insignificant change, but inside me there has been a profound changes since I first purchased that ring five years ago. Let me explain.

At the time that I purchased the ring, I felt like life was going to change because I had a feeling that my parents might not live through the winter and I was going to have to deal with everything this would entail. Life was going to give me some challenges and I was going to have to dig deep to get through this time period. Life was happening "to me". Things would be "coming at me". I felt inside that there wasn't going to be much I would be able to do about anything that happened. I wasn't in control. I would sit and wait to see what happened. Inside, I felt that life was going to be like a truck moving full throttle with a lot of momentum. There was no way that I could slow it down. I would just wait for it to hit me. One truck at a time. I would deal with whatever happened when it happened. I thought that life was going to throw some difficult things at me.

Fast forward to writing my first book. I was scared to share my story and I never would have guessed how it changed my life and my thinking. Tara, a friend, who read my book, sent me a copy of *The Untethered Soul The Journey Beyond Yourself* by Michael A. Singer. I had no idea how this one book would change my thinking, which prompted me to switch my ring facing outward instead of toward me.

**"Come to know the one who watches the voice, and you will come to know one of the great mysteries of creation." ~ Michael A. Singer**

The voice inside my head had taken over my life. I wanted to get away from this voice. I had many readers approach me and say, "I thought I was the only one who thought like that!" I also got questions from friends who wondered if I was ok now. I began questioning my entire thought process.

Here is one of my favorite sections from Michael's book,

**"Basically, you're not alone in there. There are two distinct aspects of your inner being. The first is you, the awareness, the witness, the center of your willful intentions; and the other is that which you watch. The problem is, the part that you watch never shuts up. If you could get rid of that part, even for a moment, the peace and serenity would be the nicest vacation you've ever had." ~ Michael L. Singer**

I had been busy thinking that life was happening "to me" and that I needed to respond to everything. I was in reaction mode and most of the time I felt like I needed to protect myself. This is a normal human component but sometimes in life it just isn't helpful. This was a way to run from my fears by trying to protect my psyche, as Michael calls it. I discovered I wanted out of this way of thinking.

Since Tara had recommended this book to me, I figured that I would also listen to his other book, *The Surrender Experiment,* at the same time I was reading the first book.

In his book *The Surrender Experiment,* Michael applies his work from *The Untethered Soul* and reflects on his life choices. He explains how he let life happen instead of forcing something arbitrarily. He walked us through life events where he was able to let go and let life happen. Never, in a million years, would he have guessed that life would lead him in the direction it did.

I saw many similarities in my own life. When I let life flow and wrote the book I felt called to write, it led me in a different career direction than I ever imagined!

**"Sometimes it's just tricky to hear what is being said before your head comes in and doubts it all. To differentiate the crazy voice from the wholehearted, enlightened, centered voice of your soul."** ~ Rebecca Campbell

The same is true for my career path. I never would have dreamed that I would use my training as a teacher to write a book. All of the writing courses that my principal had forced me to take (which I was very unhappy about at the time!), would give me the necessary skills to turn my dime story into a book.

The ring faces the other way now because I am open to whatever the universe brings my way. I seriously don't know what is next for me. As I enjoy my time as a Curriculum Director, I know that writing has led me in a different direction. I seek answers in a different way. I ask the universe for guidance and am curious to learn more. I am a certified Health and Life Coach (through www.healthcoachinstitute.com) and hope to be able to help others find their true soul calling and life path; one that might be different than they originally planned!

Last summer I went blueberry picking with a friend and her granddaughter. To get to the field, we had to drive on a path through the woods. There were two forks in the road and both times I went the wrong way. I had to turn around and go back. My friend and I said to each other, "Seems like they would have some signs for people to know where to go." Her granddaughter speaks up and says, "They did. Didn't you see the arrows?" Often, young children notice signs more than adults do. Honestly, I was too busy looking at the path and thinking about other things in my head. I didn't see the signs that were clearly marked.

*Was life like that sometimes? We are so busy planning our path that we forget to look at the signs from the universe all around us? Was I so busy planning my career that I didn't listen to Spirit whispering in my*

*ear? Did the universe have a different plan for me- one that I would have no way of knowing what would come next? Would I need to trust that the universe was working its magic and that if I was patient enough, it would guide me in the right direction?*

At 51 years old, I feel like I am beginning my path toward a more passionate, fulfilling work as a Health and Life Coach, Speaker, Editor, Writer, and Educator.

**"And if you want to build deeper personal or professional relationships and be a more effective change maker, you have to show up honestly and vulnerably in your life - for your colleagues, your kids, and everyone else in your world. Your story can influence and inspire someone - perhaps many people - and it can expand your understanding of your own experiences and values." ~ Heather Box and Julian Mocine-McQueen**

<u>**Questions to Ponder**</u>

- What has your career path been like?
- Do you wake up each day excited to go to work? If yes, what excites you? If no, why not?
- What are you passionate about?
- What are your dreams?
- What job would you have that wouldn't feel like work?
- What has happened in your life that you might want to write about?
- How would your story help the next person?
- Try writing something (anything!) and see where it leads you.

**"I allow my fingers to be taken over by the energy of what my heart most needs to hear." ~ Rebecca Campbell**

-

# Chapter Two:  Weeds or Flowers?

Recently I was at a conference for work. It was summertime in Vermont and I was admiring all of the beautiful flowers at the resort. The gardener was there as I walked to the conference. I commented, "The flowers are so beautiful!" She replied, "Thank you." But then she added, "There are so many weeds though!" I stopped to look. I hadn't seen the weeds until she pointed them out to me. I know that that is her job but I couldn't help but wonder about weeds and flowers in life.

Trust me when I say that I had to work through a lot of weeds in my first book to get to any of the flowers that you saw in *Dimes from Heaven*. I started writing and it opened up a door that led to things I didn't really know or understand. Later on, I would form it into chapters and sections. At the beginning, I just wrote and wrote and wrote some more! I didn't stop to think or analyze any of it. I didn't spell words correctly. I didn't have paragraphs or any structure. It was a very cathartic experience for me. It came from deep within me and I let it flow.

**"As Jesus said, 'It's the Spirit that gives life,' and words on a page appearing out of nowhere are a result of the dance of creation." ~ Dr. Wayne Dyer**

Whenever I told my dime story, people were always amazed by it! My Dad had given me a unique dime from his coin collection. Because of this coin, I would always know that dimes were a sign from him. I could tell that most people believed in signs from heaven. *Would my story be better if they knew every conversation I had with my Dad?* I usually never had time to tell them the story about the minister on the mountain, but that was pretty spectacular too!

My goal was to share all of the pieces and parts of the dime story and weave in all of the learning from all of the different books I had read. I would be able to give the reader tips on how to change their lives for the better. My story had the power to transform and give people the information to live differently - better and happier lives.

Right from the moment I put pen to paper, my story was "More Than a Dime". I knew that I had more to share than "just" my dime story. I had been reading books about healing through emotional work for years and I knew that other people didn't have the time or the opportunity to read as much as I did. I saw so many people in pain and wanted them to feel better. **If only people knew that what they think in their head has such an impact on their physical health!** This information could be transformational to millions! I wanted the people in my community to know and understand Louise Hay's messages about how our emotions affect our physical bodies. This was now a topic we were discussing in the educational world with the Adverse Childhood Experiences (ACE) study. My personal passion was meeting up with my professional world. More and more we were discussing emotional health in education- for the teachers, students and families. Now was the perfect time to use my dime story as a way to draw the reader in to learn more about how to heal in a very different way than the American medical system says we should heal.

I also wanted people to believe in signs from Heaven. I knew if they heard my dime story even the non-believers would most likely believe. I had a pretty clear vision of my message, but the process of writing took a lot of twists and turns. In this early phase of writing, I asked the universe for clarity and was given many messages. While I wrote about believing in Heaven, I began to feel sensations in my body as I wrote about events.

**"Good morning, This is God. I will be handling all of your problems today. I will not need Your help, so have A miraculous day." ~ Dr. Wayne Dyer**

Wayne Dyer speaks of writing first thing in the morning, because that is the time when we are close to Spirit, the place we visit while we are asleep. This is my best time to write. I get up at 3:00 or 4:00 in the morning and write for as long as possible. My mind is clear and fresh. I had no road map for my first book. Ideas would come when my mind was clear. To clear my mind, I exercise, do yoga and eat healthy, whole foods. Junk food equaled junk thoughts so it was important to cleanse my body from processed foods.

**"I have been writing day and night for almost a year now. The words come fast and furious, flowing freely like water from a spigot that continues to flow because of a broken pipeline. I can't plug the leak - I've never known such intensity in my writing. It comes in the middle of the night, it comes in the afternoon, and it comes in the evening as well." ~ Dr. Wayne Dyer**

My first draft was messy and I wrote in a journal instead of on a computer. I spilled lots and lots of weeds before my writing turned into the book. An example of a "weed" that I removed from my writing was the part about buying my Grandmother's house. I had originally added, "Looking back, I see now it was a way for my mother to control me." I filtered that "weed" out and realized I was blaming someone else for what I felt to be true. Judgments divide us and I didn't need to listen to that voice inside me that always judges each experience I have in life. This was me beginning to look within myself instead of judging my Mom.

For me, my writing was better if I wrote it out by hand and then transcribed it to the computer. That way, I could "weed" out some of the things that were important for me to write about to heal, but didn't necessarily need to be shared with the world!

Ideas would pop into my head in the middle of a run or when I was in a meditation. It was like as soon as my mind surrendered and quieted, messages were whispered to my soul. Ideas that I never could have come up with my conscious mind.

I've always wondered who determines which plants are weeds and which plants we call flowers. It seems as though we shouldn't have to sort them and instead be in awe of all of the beauty that surrounds us! When you are writing, there may be some weeds that you may leave behind in your final draft. But, for your first draft, let them sit there. Enjoy them. Don't worry about them. Sometimes your soul needs to express them!

- **Weeds or Flowers?**
  * I can see flowers instead of weeds in my life.
  *I acknowledge the weeds but don't focus on them.
  * I realize that both

> weeds and flowers are important in my life. They help balance my life and keep me humble.
>
>          * I understand that it is one's perceptions and judgments that determine which we see as weeds or flowers. It's always a choice.

"Some people could be given an entire field of roses and only see the thorns in it. Others could be given a single weed and only see the wildflower in it. Perception is a key component to gratitude. And gratitude is a key component to joy." ~ Amy Wentherly

### Questions to Ponder

- What big message do you want the reader to gain from your book or story?
- What are the smaller messages within the big message?
- Sometimes people like to have outlines for their books. Decide if that feels right to you.
- When you begin writing, brainstorm around 20 different titles and subtitles. Then, don't get too attached to them. Put them aside until later.
- Write from beginning to end and don't worry about perfection. Just write and write and write some more. Don't worry if you don't know where you are going. It might appear at any moment!
- What "weeds" are you focusing on?
- What "flowers" do you see in your writing?

"We spend way too much time in filtered social media moments and not enough time in the sometimes prickly weeds of real life." ~ Heather Box and Julian Mcine-McQueen

### My Self Publishing Journey

"Once you make a decision, the Universe conspires to make it happen." ~ Ralph Waldo Emerson

April 14, 2018 - On our flight home the week I started writing my first book, I decide to finish reading a book I had started reading months earlier. Normally on vacation, I read instead of write. I had brought a few books on my trip. I like to finish things so I decided on the flight home, I would finish this particular book. I had a few chapters left. Timing is everything. The book ended with this, "Kelley makes a resolution. He is going to write a novel. And forget the Christmas letter! He's going to start right now, this instant. He doesn't have any time to waste!" (pg 243 Elin Hilderbrand's book, Winter Storms.) Those were the very last words of the book. Talk about a sign? Really?

As I wrote in Dimes From Heaven, I felt strongly that I wanted to be able to keep my story my story. I didn't want an editor or publisher to change the flow of my book. I knew this from when I started writing. A few weeks after my trip to Florida, I googled Hay House self-publishing. I knew I would be able to publish for free on Amazon, but I felt like I needed a little more support.

I discovered Balboa Press, a self publishing company that is a division of Hay House. I knew it! I knew Louise Hay would have a way for someone like me, a new author, to get published. Some other self-publishing companies are www.outskirtspress.com, www.lulu.com, https://kdp.amazon.com/en_US/ or www.bookbaby.com to name a few. The book you are now reading was done on Kindle Direct Publishing.

The first person I speak with at Balboa Press has a bunch of 5's in his extension- *immediately I feel this is a sign!* The number 5 was the number my Dad sent to my son and I on our trip to a Red Sox game. I share this with the representative. He says, "*Well, you're with Balboa now. There will always be messages. There really aren't just coincidences."*

The company asks how long it will take for me to finish my manuscript. I naively say, *"Oh, maybe a few months."* I ask my friend how long it took her to publish her young adult fiction book. *"About 10 years,"* she says. I think to myself, *"Hell no! This will not take me 10 years!"* Honestly, it did take me longer than I originally anticipated, but I was on a mission. I was ready to share my story with the world!

June 2018 - I decide to buy Louise Hay's movie You Can Heal Your Life. Right at the beginning of the movie, Louise says "I worked in a dime store." *Do I think this sign to continue writing was directly from Louise Hay? FOR SURE! A true God Wink!*

"Don't be practical. Don't think about making a living; think about doing something you love." ~ Brené Brown

3 ▌

# Chapter Three:  Seen or Unseen?

There are hidden messages everywhere and the only way to "see" them is to believe in them.

**June 30, 2018**

I chat with my friend, Tracy, on the phone. We talk about the title of my first book. We talk about my life as a teacher and how much passion and excitement I put into teaching Math. Kids and parents could feel my energy and they all start to love Math! After talking, I listen to a Hay House audio book. It is an interview with Deepak Chopra and Judith Orloff. Deepak begins by talking about how everything that God created is Mathematical and how all Mathematics come from nature. *How could this be? He was talking about Math after I finished talking with my friend. Was it a message from Deepak? For sure! Why does this happen? What does this mean? My linear, mathematical brain always wanted an explanation for everything to be proven. I didn't want any guesswork - only things that I could see would I believe in. That's the part in the story I was working on.*

Along with books, I began to notice patterns and lessons in my life. *What were the people around me teaching me? How would I use this information in my book?*

**"Faith is a place of mystery, where we find the courage to believe in what we cannot see and the strength to let go of our fear of uncertainty." ~ Brené Brown**

I read the first three chapters of my first book to Eldon, my father's best friend. We talk about God and his beliefs throughout the time I read. Right before I read chapter three to him, he says, "Oh, that breeze feels so good." The end of chapter three is where I say, "Wait, is Faith like the wind? The wind blows but one cannot see it. We all know the wind is there because of the effects it has on other things, like leaves and flags...Is Faith like that?...Are they feeling faith blow onto them like the wind hitting their skin?" ~Monica L. Morrissey *Was there an unseen force from the universe at work here?*

Then, I tell him the name of the chapter - Faith. He says, well, what does the scripture say about faith? I smile and read the first quote from the Bible, "For we live by faith, not by sight." 2 Corinthians 5:7. He smiles and says - "You got it."

After reading some, Eldon says, "For a book about faith, you don't have much from the Bible, dear." I think- yup, he is right. I think back to the lawn sale I went to a couple of days ago. A friend told me to go because there were some really good baskets that are usually super expensive, but these were priced about half what one would normally pay. I go because she is insisting. I think maybe I'll find something for Christmas presents. I am looking around at the lawn sale. I find one basket for $10 and decide to get it. I glance down at a box of books. Inside is the book, *The Secret*. I had read this book years ago but couldn't find my copy. I grab it up and then dig into the box some more. I find several books about God and notice one in particular. I think of this book as Eldon tells me I don't have enough information from the Bible. It is called *Never Lose Heart* by Joyce Meyer. I also wonder if Eldon's wife, Joyce, was trying to send me a message. Was she one of my cheerleaders in Heaven; helping me believe that I was meant to publish my book? Only if I believe!

**"You are learning, growing, and discovering the tools you will need for the manifestation. The fun is walking on the path. When you go for a hike in the mountains, you don't ask to jump to the top, right? You walk each step of the trail and see the plants,**

animals, rocks, and enjoy being out in nature. The same applies to the steps we take toward our goals." ~ Maureen Scanlon

I continued to read books that were put in my path. *I felt like there was something missing. Something I was searching for and hadn't discovered yet.* I also began to gather quotes from a variety of authors. I re-read books to see if there were messages for me. I looked for evidence to back up some of my story. *What were other authors saying about our connection to Heaven or past life regression work?*

I decide that I want to go to a Brian Weiss event as part of my research.

**"As a traditional psychotherapist, Dr. Brian Weiss was astonished and skeptical when one of his patients began recalling past-life traumas that seemed to hold the key to her recurring nightmares and anxiety attacks. His skepticism was eroded, however, when she began to channel messages from "the space between lives," which contained remarkable revelations about Dr. Weiss's family and his dead son. Using past-life therapy, he was able to cure the patient and embark on a new, more meaningful phase of his own career."**
www.brianwiess.com

Brian Weiss followed his internal guidance when presented with a different way of thinking about what our human experience is really about. He was willing to change his beliefs and ultimately change the course of millions of people. *How would it feel to be a traditional doctor now believing in things that some people think are nonsense?* I wanted to understand this concept more.

I buy a ticket and decide that it was my gift to myself for my 50th birthday! His book was the book that had inspired me after my nephew, Tyler, passed away suddenly. Tyler was only 21 years old when he transitioned to Spirit. He is my reminder that life is not promised and we need to cherish every single day. I know Tyler is always around during every baseball game where his good friend, David Price, is pitching. He is also around every time the number eight appears in my life.

Maybe I would get some insight if I went to see Brian Weiss in person. I knew there was another presenter who was also going to be there, but I had no idea who that was. I only cared about seeing Brian. Well, the universe sure knew that I needed to hear John Holland that day too!

John Holland is a medium with a lot of experience in the Spirit world. That day, I gained an understanding of what a medium was and was not. His presentation and books would help me describe how messages from Heaven are received.

On the way to Boston to see Brian Weiss, some friends and I stop to shop. Tracy and Chelsea, long time friends, decided to join me on my trip. They are now an integral part of my team and I am so thankful they are in my life.

**"I feel as if a warm shower is running inside of me, which I often call 'the tinglies.' ~ Dr. Wayne Dyer**

We all buy Converse sneakers and wear them while we shop. When we get to the hotel, Tracy takes a picture of the sneakers. She posts the picture on Facebook and asks me for a good quote to go with her post. I brought chapters one through four of my book for them to read. I thought of my nephew, Tyler's poem at the end of Chapter four in *Dimes from Heaven,* but didn't want to spoil their reading for the night. Here is his poem:

*"His Road Not Taken*
*Going along the path,*

*There's a split in my way*
*Which way should I choose?*
*I will find out another day.*
*The two paths are different,*
*I don't know which one to choose.*
*One seems to be very new,*
*The other has been stomped on by shoes."*
                    *By Tyler Morrissey March 7, 2001*

She posted the picture with something from Dr. Seuss about "Oh the Places You'll Go!" But in my head, I was thinking, "Which way should I choose?" or "The two paths are different, I don't know which one to choose?" from Tyler's poem. *After they read the chapters, I mention it to them - the significance of the shoes and the poem. That's "CRAZY", we say as we laugh, get goosebumps and tingle feelings all over our bodies!*

We are walking in Boston trying to find the venue for the "Journey of the Soul" day with Brian Weiss and John Holland. We happened upon James St. (my Dad's name was James) right after I see a gray squirrel running in the street. My Dad's bird feeder was for the gray squirrels too! I mention it and we all agree that street helped us find our way to the venue. *A message from my Dad?*

While we were waiting for the speaker to begin, Chelsea pulls up her memories on Facebook. We had recently joked about me telling her to write a book, but we couldn't remember when I had started to tell her that. *She was my boomerang advice. Boomerang advice is advice that I give to others that really should be advice I give to myself.* It's what I need to hear! She opens up the comments on one of her posts from exactly one year ago. Here is her post: **"Unf*@k yourself. Be who you were before all that stuff happened that dimmed your f*@king shine."** And, my comment was, "Is that the title to your new book you need to write? I'd buy it!" It was exactly one year ago that I told her to write a book!

It was my birthday the day after the workshop. During the presentation Brian Weiss thanked Hay House for supporting this event. *I thought in my head, yes - thank God for Hay House and Louise Hay! Because of her and her dreams, I was going to be able to self publish my book! Then Brian said, "And it is Louise's birthday tomorrow!"* **Louise Hay and I have the same birth date!** *Well, let's be honest- different years but the SAME DAY! Did I take this as another sign? You bet! Louise was cheering me on to continue writing.*

### July 2, 2018

I order a book from Amazon today. Just out of curiosity I track the item to see where it was shipping from (something I never usually do). It is shipping from **Goodyear,** Arizona. My Father ran a Goodyear dealership for years. *Really? I think. There is actually a town named Goodyear?* This message might not have been **seen** if I hadn't listened to my intuition when it said, "Hey, let's track this book!" It wasn't what I usually did but I decided to do it just for fun!

**"Start before you feel ready. You don't need to know where it's all going. You'll work it out along the way." ~ Rebecca Campbell**

Once I started writing, there seemed to be this unseen force where everything around me began to listen to what I was thinking or writing about. The signs would appear out of nowhere and although no one else would know, I knew that all of the coincidences and synchronicities were being coordinated by the universe to help me along my journey.

**"I know when I am writing from my soul as my whole energy changes, my writing style shifts slightly and it feels like I am being pulled by a gentle current in a deep, warm ocean." ~ Rebecca Campbell**

**Seen or Unseen?**

There can be hidden messages everywhere. I have to believe in them to see them.

I had to follow my intuition (unseen thoughts, feelings, and guidance) in order for the signs to be seen. I also had to ask my Angels, Spirit guides, and God for help. They are always there - we have to be willing to ask for help in order for them to support us!

## Questions to Ponder

- Discover what other people say about your topic.
- What have other people written about? Many people most likely have written about the topic you are writing about. How will yours be different or unique?
- Are there any quotes that might help your writing? These should support either your smaller or bigger messages.
- Watch for signs from the universe - these can be anywhere! Something pops up on Facebook or a commercial on TV. Get curious and find the meaning in the messages.
- Meditate. Sometimes our research and guidance comes from deep within us - from our soul. It wants to help you!
- If stuck, talk to someone OR go to bed and ask your guides to help supply you with a direction. When you wake up, write about your dream - even if it doesn't make sense! It might make sense later on or if you think about your dreams as a metaphor or an analogy. What was the story in your dream trying to communicate?
- What is your intuition telling you?

## My Self Publishing Journey
**"Your job is to work out the what. The Universe's job is to work out the how." ~ Rebecca Campbell**

*A Stitch in Time* by Daphne Kalmar was released in the town where I live. It was a young adult novel that takes place in Vermont in the early 1900's. I knew Daphne personally as we had worked together years ago. I went to her book release night and asked a few questions about the process. It took her ten years to write her book! And, to get an agent or a publisher is next to impossible! This made me nervous about how long it would take me to finish writing my book. The one big piece of advice she said that night was she had to figure out that the book was really about grief. I went home and thought about that a lot. *Was my story about grief?* I didn't think it was, but, if it wasn't about grief, then what was it about? I decide that night I need to ask for guidance- I went to bed and asked out loud- *"What is the main theme of my book?"*

Answers can come in mysterious ways! The very next morning, my older sister, Debbie, sends me a picture of a cute puppy she wants to adopt. I reply, *"Awesome! What is her/his name?"* Her response, *"I'm thinking Faith, but not sure right now."*

*Is this what my book is about? Do I need Faith in order to believe? And, exactly what do I believe? I had to be willing to "see" this as an answer to my question.* My sister did end up getting the puppy, but she didn't name it Faith. She had given me part of my answer to the theme of my book! When I zeroed in on that, it helped me with my entire book.

### Turning a Story into a Book
Another part of the research phase was reading books by authors who had a style of writing that I liked. I had to figure out who I was as a writer, not just a storyteller. It helped me go from telling a story to having the person feel like they were a part of my story.

I had a good story to tell, but had no idea how to turn it into a book. An opportunity through Hay House for an online Writer's Workshop course appeared in my email. The cost was $699 but was valued at over $2,000! I was hesitant. I searched for other online writing classes and discovered that some of them were over $5,000. Since I loved Hay House and trusted them, I bought the course. I never once regretted that purchase. It led me to things I could never have imagined! I even met and spoke with Reid Tracy, the CEO of Hay House!

When I want to learn something new, I am curious and I'll do whatever it takes. I began watching all of the online videos for the Writer's Workshops while running on the treadmill. I would have my computer set up on top of the treadmill and keep clicking through them all! Through this course, I not only became a better writer, but I learned more about what it meant to be an author. From social media training to book releases to the publishing industry, Hay House was where I learned the most about the process. I learned how to turn my story into a book and how to build my marketing platform.

"When you follow what you love, the Universe will pick up on your expanded feelings and send you more things to match your newly found expansion." ~ Rebecca Campbell

# Chapter Four: Connected or Disconnected?

"In my research, I found that what silences our intuitive voice is our need for certainty...And there it is. *'What does your gut say?'* We shake our head and say, 'I'm not sure' when the real answer is, *'I have no idea what my gut says; we haven't spoken in years."* ~ Brené Brown

I had no idea how disconnected I was from my physical body until I began to slow down. When I began to meditate, I realized that I avoided outwardly feeling emotions and was in my head much more than I realized. I was busy judging others and reacting to every little thing that happened. Life was easier this way because then I can numb any feelings I have. By doing this though, I was disconnected from everything in my life.

**August 3, 2018**

I had been reading Dr. Christian Northrup's book about menopause and aging. She cited several studies about positive thinking and how it affects your body as you age. *How would this information work its way into my book?*

**"I wish that more women would realize the degree to which their musculoskeletal problems - be they with shoulders, hips, neck, or back - have an emotional basis. Simply acknowledging this possibility opens up huge vistas of healing. ~ Dr. Christian Northrup**

At some point, I had heard that hip pain is related to male and female energy, and possibly your parents. I was on a pretty challenging hike this day and was thinking negative thoughts. As I was heading down the mountain, with everyone way ahead of me, in the pouring rain, I was thinking things like, *"My knees hurt. My hip hurts. I am going to be so sore after this. My ankle feels weak. "* And many, many more negative thoughts. Then, I became aware of my negative self talk and I thought of Louise Hay and Dr. Christian Northrup - both of them turning negative thoughts into positive affirmations. My frame of mind changes to, *"My hips are strong and stable. I have strong muscles around my knees. I flow down the mountain with ease and strength." I was trying to think of something similar to Dr. Northrup's "programming" her mind:*

**"My body is now radiantly healthy, beautiful, flexible, strong, and eternally youthful. The spirit of Divine Love and Power now manifests throughout my entire body as radiant health, radiant beauty, and radiant youth. I give thanks that my body, mind, spirit, and behavior now align to easily maintain my ideal size and weight." ~ Dr. Christian Northrup.**

I'm hiking with my husband and another couple. It is raining and beginning to thunder. They are way ahead of me and I can't even see them. My shoes are extremely slippery and at times I need to slide on my bottom just to navigate the trail. I begin to get angry. The trail is difficult and, even though I don't want to admit it, I may need help and I wished that my husband was there with me. The old me would have been fuming the entire way and never would have admitted that I wanted or needed help. Instead, I stop and text him. *"Would you please wait up for me?"*

Within minutes, I see him stopped at the trail, waiting for me. Simple as that. All I had to do was ask and he was there. *How would he have known that I wanted his help if I never asked?* He proceeds to help me down the challenging parts of the trail.

This is when I begin my positive self talk. "*I am strong. I have strong hips. I will not be like my mother who did not stay active. I am changing my DNA footprint and creating a new, stronger one. I will succeed and be more active than my mother.*" At one point, he offers me a hand as I am trying to place my foot on the next step off a high rock. He pauses and points. There is a penny in the middle of the trail on the same rock I am about to put my foot on.

*For real? I believe pennies are a sign from my Mom. This is how my mother shows herself to me? In the middle of the trail? When I am in the middle of doing positive self talk and getting totally freaked out because I know there are more challenging parts in the trail coming up soon?* We pick up the penny and I ask my husband to keep it for me. *He has absolutely NO idea what has just been going through my head.* That penny gave me the courage and strength to get through some steep parts of the trail when I was scared and nervous. I felt a tipping point - I knew that I needed to be exercising more and making sure to stay strong as my body ages. I also needed to get back to my writing. This was me practicing using some of the research I was reading about. *I knew that I would somehow have to work positive affirmations into the book and my life. And, I knew, my mother was helping me.*

Another "coincidence" happened when I watch Louise Hay's movie, *"You Can Heal Your Life."* Dr. Christian Northrup talks about "jumping in front of a car" because it would be "easier" than life. In *Dimes From Heaven*, I share that during my first year of college I wanted to run my car head on into a tree. I thought life would be easier if I wasn't here. Dr. Northrup showed me another sign for me to continue writing my story and share some of most intimate thoughts. I hoped that by sharing my story, people would see that everyone struggles for a sense of belonging. *Most people who look at me from the outside most likely believe that I am fine on the inside. I wanted people to be more understanding and treat people with more kindness because we don't know everyone's story. By sharing my story, it would make it a safe place for others to share their story. Dr. Chrisitan Northrup helped give me the courage to share.*

I was still focused on the four main ideas of my book 1. Messages from Heaven (the dimes) 2. Loving myself (Anita Moorjani), 3. Healing with emotions (Louise Hay) and 4. Past Life Regressions (Brian Weiss). I had yet to discover anything about being an empath. I was curious and I was beginning to connect into something that I had been disconnected from for a long, long time - **my intuition, the universe's positive energy and the secret portal where there is an unseen force that we are all connected to.**

Connected or Disconnected?
- I know I was connected to Spirit while writing.
- I felt disconnected from my body.
- I began to learn to be connected to my body through meditation and practicing mindfulness.
- In the past, I disconnected from myself with food, alcohol, and avoiding my feelings.
- I was beginning to connect back to the light within myself.

### Questions to Ponder:

- What part of your story resonates with you the most?
- How will you use this information to move your writing forward?
- What pieces (if any) are you missing?
- Continue to gather information and integrate it into your story.
- Connect with your gut. What does it say?
- Who can read your book/story for honest feedback? Make sure you tell them it is safe to share their honest opinion.

**"By not addressing what's going on inside us, we often find ourselves stuck and feeling limited. But by simply rearranging our**

priorities, we can release the internal change needed to begin the external result." ~ Lisa Marie Runfola

## My Self Publishing Journey

*I run on the beach and reflect on my writing. A storm has come through during the night. It changed the look of the beach. Before, there was a red, slimy, thick seaweed all over the beach. Now, the waves are bigger and the wind from the storm has stayed a while longer. The sun glimmers on the new beachfront. The red seaweed is all gone. It is replaced with green, grasslike weeds. Writing my book was like a storm. I'm on the other side and I can reflect on my journey. I can see now that my years of teaching writing helped me become an author. I can see that I had to face my fears in order to share my story.*

It's important to figure out what type of help you need in your writing. There are two types of editing services. One is for content and structure. The other is for grammar, usage and mechanics. Both are critical to the writing process. It's important to figure out which one you need and how to get it without spending a fortune. When I investigated into professional editing services, the cost was extreme. I had friends help me. I know that as I transition into being an author and coach full-time, I will most likely be providing some of these services. Because I taught writing for so many years, I have the necessary skills to help others and I look forward to helping the next person write their story!

Because I was a teacher, my editing process was most likely not the normal process. I read my drafts over and over and over again. Chapters began forming and when I thought I had it close to being done, I called a friend to help. Kim looked for spelling, verb tense, transitions, story elements, and clear, precise, descriptive language. We went over my manuscript several times.

Sharing with people is critical to the writing process. The first time I read part of my original manuscript to a friend, I was extremely nervous. Just before Vicki arrived, I was sitting outside on my front porch and my voice was born. I wrote the section where I found the dime on the mountain. The italicized writing and questions flowed like never before. I was becoming a writer instead of a storyteller. I had found my voice. The reader would hear my internal thoughts, a way for them to experience the story right along with me.

I heard feedback from several readers about that voice inside my head. My cousin texted me and said, "Your book was delivered a little over an hour ago and I haven't put it down!!! It's an incredible, courageous journey. So far, I LOVE it! So much is happening inside of me. I can't explain." Another friend said, "Somehow I feel lighter after reading your book." Someone else would send a "Thank you so much for writing your book. Somehow I feel different."

Using the internal voice and asking myself questions within the dime story was helping the readers activate their metacognition, requiring them to not only think about my story but apply the questions to their own life. They were thinking about their thinking as I shared my internal dialogue.

Toward the end of the process, I thought about who would want to read my book. I phoned a few close friends and asked them to read my book to see if they liked it. They were reading it for the content and storyline. The question would be, "*Did the story make you want to keep reading the book?*" That's the sign of a true good book! One where the reader doesn't want to stop reading!

I had to be open to constructive criticism but also listen to my intuition. I had to make decisions of whether or not to listen to their advice or stay with my ideas. While one friend didn't like all of the quotes; another friend told me she loved the quotes! I had to decide for myself what felt right to me.

**"My creations uplift and inspire people all around the world. I serve the world by being me."** ~ Rebecca Campbell

Sometimes we have to feel the disconnection before we learn how to truly connect. It was important for me to disconnect from the negative voice inside myself who was filled with fear. It was important for me to connect in a lot of different ways. I felt that pain in my body was a way for me to connect to my physical body. Pain brings a person into the present moment. I had to learn to connect with the environment around me to feel the power of the universe, especially in nature. Writing and sharing most definitely helped me connect more authentically with people in my life.

"I write extensively on the specifics of moving from an ego-based identity with its focus on competition, fear, and outward appearances; to higher awareness such as peace, truth, love, and purity." ~ Dr. Wayne Dyer

# Chapter Five: Subconscious or Conscious?

"Conscious thought is characterized by attempts to rationalize based on structure and logic and forced inhibitions because of social constraints."

"Subconscious thoughts flow freely, uninhibited, as in a dream, and usually reflect on the deeper feelings you have or emotions you feel biologically and physically."

retrieved from https://www.quora.com/What-is-the-difference-between-conscious-and-subconscious-mind-in-simple-terms

Our subconscious mind controls about 90% of our thoughts while our conscious mind controls only about 10%. In education, we talk about the "hidden or societal curriculum" --as defined by Cortes, 1981, "the massive, ongoing, informal curriculum of family, peer groups, neighborhoods, churches, organizations, occupations, mass media and other socializing forces that 'educate' all of us throughout our lives." I compare that to our subconscious programming. Our subconscious controls our beliefs, emotions, habits, values, protective reactions, long term memory, imagination, and intuition that we learned at a very young age, when the world was very different and we were so young that we didn't know we were absorbing the feelings of those around us. Some of the feelings and thoughts of past generations are no longer useful in our society. Our experiences in life determine all of these things. Our conscious mind is filled with will power, long term thinking, logical and critical thinking. We all have learned to navigate the "societal curriculum" of life in both our subconscious and conscious thinking.

While writing, my subconscious and conscious supported me along my journey. I would have dreams and wake up with messages. I had to figure out what the dream was trying to tell me. *What information did I want to include and what was extraneous information that didn't quite fit?* My conscious self began to hear messages from my subconscious and I began to form "sandwiches" of topics within each chapter. The beginning and the end of each chapter had a message that clearly gave the reader a topic or idea to think about. The name of the chapters came after I wrote them!

### June 2018

I have two bunny rabbits that live near my house. I often see them, especially while driving down my long driveway. Last year whenever I saw them, I always thought to myself, *"Chase your dreams. Chase your dreams." Like the bunnies running away, I envisioned the next part of my life. At this time last year, I was interviewing for a new job and was trying to chase my dreams. This year, as I write, I am chasing my dream to publish my book!* **"Chase my dreams. Chase my dreams," *a voice whispers as I watch the bunnies jump away.*** *My subconscious helping push my conscious mind.*

I let my writing sit. I walked away. I didn't look at my writing for weeks. I went swimming, hiking and enjoyed watching my son marry the woman of his dreams. I enjoyed my friends and family. I let my book "cook". I was worried about some of the things I had written about my parents. They weren't horrible; but they weren't good either.

At the time, I thought I was procrastinating. Mel Robbins, in her book *The Five Second Rule* explains there are two different types of procrastination. I thought I was doing it out of fear. Like Mel says in her book,

**"Procrastination can easily become a habit. In the early stages of building my own company years ago, I used to procrastinate due to the fear of rejection." ~ Mel Robbins.**

Then she goes on to explain that there is an intentional type of procrastination that is part of the creative process. Here is what she says:

**"Use Productive Procrastination: Big projects at work or things *like writing your first book* can take a lot of time and energy. Sometimes you need to step back and take a break from the problem to let the answer find you.**

**Don't be afraid to use "productive procrastination" to help you solve a big problem. It might take a few days or even a few weeks but often times a break is just what you need to get clear and find a new solution." ~ Mel Robbins**

Seriously, I didn't know I was doing this! I thought I was avoiding my writing because I was scared! I can see now that I was supposed to do this and I didn't need to feel guilty about it!

**June 17, 2018**

It's Father's Day. My sister posts a picture on Facebook of me, her and our father. I am about one and a half years old in the picture. I am lying on top of my father's chest on the floor. That same morning I take a walk with a friend and find a penny. The year on it is 1969, which would be about the time the picture was taken. *A message from both of my parents? My mother always sends pennies, but the picture was me and my dad!*

When I originally hired Balboa Press to publish my book, I told them I would have my manuscript ready in a few months. *What was I doing? I was letting my book just sit there. I needed to work night and day to get this done! My conscious brain trained for so long to finish whatever I start. A voice inside whispered, "Remember your action research - enjoy the journey and don't worry about 'finishing'." I listened but felt a stirring inside me, willing me to eventually get back to writing.* **"Time does** *change your perspective."* ~ *Monica L. Morrissey  I knew something wasn't quite right but didn't know how to fix it.*

Through meditation, I went deeper into my subconscious and more miracles began to happen. My mind was relaxed and stories came to me to support my ideas. Metaphors like the boots compared to relationships began to appear out of nowhere. I had to learn to relax and allow the thoughts to come. It wasn't my linear brain focused on completing my book project.

**"No matter your family history or what you've been through, what you choose to do today has the greatest effect on your tomorrow." ~ Dr. Mike Dow**

Every time I read something I had written about my mother, I got this sick feeling and felt ashamed that I was talking badly about her. I remember a phone call I had with a medium once. I said I was struggling with my mother. She responded something like, *"You feel bad because a lot of people seem to really like your Mom."* I was like, "Yes!" She understood. My Mom was super nice to my friends and the customers at our family business. *I knew I had to dig deep into this relationship and this could eventually be part of my healing process.*

When we got home from a camping trip the summer I was writing, I went to a friend's house. Their daughter had been taking care of our dog while we were away. I wanted to pay and thank her. While chatting with them, their four kids are all playing. I notice the woman's shirt, "Faith over Fear"- what I almost named my first book. Interesting... Then, the two boys are playing on the stairs. A coin mysteriously appears out of nowhere and gets knocked down the stairs. I immediately look to see what it is - you guessed it - a dime! Nobody noticed the dime, but I knew that I had seen a sign.

**"Your soul is always calling you in the direction of your wholeness, flow, dreams and purpose (and everything else). But, you have to show up to it to hear it." ~ Rebecca Campbell**

*This is a reminder to get going on the "project" you told your friend, Jessie, about at the wedding last night. We were talking about following* *our inner guidance from our soul; the thing we feel passionate about. I told her that I had a "project" that I was working on because I didn't think I had the energy to become a principal. I expected that being a principal would take over my entire physical health, making me ill and I just didn't think that was what I wanted to do with my life. The demands that a principal faces nowadays are impossible for one person to be able to do. When I said I had a "project", but wasn't ready to share about it, her eyes lit up and she said, "That's it. That's what you are supposed to do. I don't have any idea what **that** is, but **that** is what you are supposed to do. Do it. Tell people about it. That's your answer." The extra dime was a reminder for me to get doing **that!***

*I had taken a break from my writing, but all of these signs sent me back to working on my book!*

I let go and let God help lead the way. I had to release my fears to the universe and trust that I was supposed to more forward to publish my book.

**"You are the consciousness that is behind the mind and is aware of the thoughts." ~ Michael A. Singer**

**Subconscious vs Conscious**
- My subconscious mind was rewiring and changing my internal belief system.
- My conscious mind was helping me accomplish the tasks needed in order to publish my book.
- My subconscious mind sent me messages in my dreams and thoughts and wanted to express my creativity.
- My conscious mind was worried about what others might think or say.
- My subconscious mind knew that I was being called to write a book.

"You are capable of ceasing the absurdity of listening to the perpetual problems of your psyche." ~ Micheal A. Singer

<u>Questions to Ponder:</u>

- Walk away from your writing. Run, plan, exercise, spend time with people. Whatever you do, just don't consciously think about your writing. Use productive procrastination.
- Connect with your gut about the material so far. It will guide you. Should you keep writing more or do you need to work on what you already have?
- Have you truly relayed to the reader what you set out to in the beginning?
- If your message is different than your original thoughts, what happened? What changed? How do you feel about this?
- Think of who your reader is and pretend your book is talking directly to them. What would they say?
- Who do you have that can read your book and give you feedback?
- Do you know anyone that will help you with editing?

Mantra: "My creations uplift and inspire people all around the world. I serve the world by being me." ~ Rebecca Campbell

---

### My Self Publishing Journey

It's important to share your story with others to get honest feedback. If real people are in your book, make sure to get permission to use their name before you publish. Some people may request their name to be changed so they won't be identified.

*Another coincidence happened during this phase. Since Merrilee was in the book so much, I wanted her to read the entire book. I knew she would be totally honest with me and since she knew my Dad so well, she would give me good advice. I went to her house and she was*

---

*so excited! Her husband, Don, was there too. She begs me to read the first chapter to her.*

*Her husband mutes the TV and I proceed to read to both of them. At the end of the chapter, Don replies, "Hmmmm..... The guy on TV was just holding up a huge dime...." Merrilee and I gasp and say, "What do you mean?" We rewind the program and can't believe our eyes! I snap a quick picture on my phone that shows a big plastic dime about 10 inches in diameter. It is attached to a stick. My Dad was getting pretty clever with the messages now!*

I submitted the 1st copy of my manuscript on Tuesday, January 8th, 2019. Most companies will want your manuscript as one document, preferably using Microsoft Word. Some writers use the program Scrivener to help organize their work. (https://www.literatureandlatte.com/scrivener/overview) I chose to first put all of my chapters on separate Google documents in one folder. When I felt they were all ready, I uploaded them into a Word document. In Scrivener, the program organizes your chapters and outline for you so you can easily transition and move things around.

I emailed my book consultant and asked what the timeline was now that they had my manuscript. She responded, "It will take our readers about 2-3 weeks to read your book. After that they will recommend what type of editing services you will need." From the Hay House Online writer's course, I knew that most writers don't think they need editing services, but they really do! I sat back and waited to hear from them.

The package I purchased from Balboa included the following: ISBN number, Copyright registration, Library of Congress registration, Book Sellers return program, and editorial assessment.

On Monday the very next week, the company sends me the book proof - a layout of the book with all of the pictures included. I was so confused! They had said 2-3 weeks and that I would have to have an editor of some kind. *This was 3 business days later and no discussion of an editor. I had no idea that this was not normal! Well, I guess I'll just go with it; what else was I supposed to do?*

I highly suggest Kelly Notaras's book The Book You Were Born to Write or Joni B. Cole's book Good Naked. Both have helpful techniques for writing a book!

"If the subconscious is your iPhone's cloud-based memory with limitless storage potential, the conscious is the small 8 GB memory on the phone itself, with a limited amount of videos, pictures, and apps it can hold at any one time. I wonder how the power of imagery, visualization, and rehearsal will empower you to take control of your life and take action." ~ Dr. Mike Dow

## Chapter Six:  Mindfulness or Mindfullness?

**"And, when you want something, all the universe conspires in helping you to achieve it."** ~ Paulo Coelho

"Quantum leaps come from your soul," Deepak Chopra speaks to me. "All creativity is based on quantum leaps and uncertainty." ~ Deepak Chopra.

This "in-spires" you to speak from spirit. As Wayne Dyer points out, Inspiration comes from Latin and means "In-spirit".

**A Quantum leap is about to get real......**

My mind had been so full. When I let myself relax, messages came and I gained a whole new perspective. A quantum leap is an abrupt change. For me, the abrupt change would be in how I viewed my life. *Had the events in my life offered me lessons to learn from?*

I make an appointment to have the woman who bought my parents' house give me a make-up lesson to prepare for a photo shoot for the book. I don't wear much make-up because of my sensitive skin. I go to her house (the house I grew up in) and we spent almost three hours chatting and doing make-up. She was amazing. It was great to see her family making our home their home. She shared with me how the first day they bought the house, she felt like she was "home". Her husband handed me a birthday card he found- It was to my Mother, from her brother (my uncle). The title was, "From ribbons to wrinkles". How funny that he had never given this to me before and, on this particular day, brings it to me. It even had a picture of my mother when she was young. *It makes me realize that I don't know my mother's young life. What made her the way she was? I was beginning to see my Mom in a different light - my book was about to change and I would make a huge quantum leap!* The card was significant to me because much of what I was going through was accepting this next part of my life - over 50 and loving life. *I wanted ribbons with my wrinkles!*

"**I define *calm* as *creating perspective and mindfulness while managing emotional reactivity.*"** ~ Brené Brown

The summer I was writing my book, I felt very alone. I had plenty of family and friends around, but I felt like I was on a journey down a new path. I was searching for my center through writing. In the body, the third chakra is located at your solar plexus (just above your belly button). Along with writing, I was adjusting my body to be more confident. The third chakra has to do with self confidence, self motivation and a strong sense of purpose. While at a conference, a woman who I met in one of the workshops says to me, "When are you expecting?" I said, "What did you just say?" She repeated the question and it took me a minute to wrap my brain about what she was asking. *She thought I was pregnant! Am I really that fat? I immediately suck in my gut and am worried about my physical appearance. I thought this dress was flattering! Does it make me look fat? Obviously, if she thought I was pregnant! I respond to her, "Um, I'm not expecting. Thanks," and quickly change the subject.* I thought about that a lot over the next few months. I sort of was pregnant - just with a book, not a baby! And, I think she was actually sensing the energy I was giving to my third chakra.

I began thinking about what it would be like to release my book to the universe. *How could I write those thing about my mother?* I read Dr. Christian Northrup's books, *The Wisdom of Menopause* and *Mother*

*Daughters.* She says that we take on our ancestor's stories - they are built into our DNA! They are built into our subconscious mind from childhood. *Had I taken on some insecurities or other things from my mother? Which she had taken on from her Mother?* Yes, but every time I re-read something that I had written about my mother, I felt a twinge in the pit of my stomach. I learned during this lifetime, insecurities was something I needed to heal. I was willing to heal myself and then this lesson ends with me. I don't have to pass it on to my children.

At some point, I stumbled upon some books about empaths. I had remembered my friend, Michelle, telling me I was an empath but hadn't really thought a lot about it. I had organized a training for teachers about compassion fatigue. During the presentation, they were talking about Highly Sensitive People. *Yikes! She is describing me. I don't even want to take the assessment to know my score. I'm sure it will be a high score. I decide that I won't focus on myself; I'll focus on the teachers. It's so much easier to help other people instead of looking within myself. I didn't want other people to know anything about this part of me.*

After this initial training, I read more about Dr. Elaine Aron's research about the highly sensitive person. Her work is based on Carl Jung's work and is most definitely helpful for anyone who thinks they might be highly sensitive or an empath.

Later, when I discovered Dr. Judith Orloff's books about being an empath, I was ready to hear the information. Or should I say - the books found me? After a good friend sent me a few audio books about surviving as an empath, *Amazon "suggested" more books about empaths to me - a sign from the universe? The one I had been searching for? The key to my understanding?*

This was the time for what Deepak Chopra calls a "Quantum leap" and I had no idea that I was actually doing it. It happened naturally, as if the universe was helping me. I was willing to look at myself as a highly sensitive person.

**"Stillness is not about focusing on nothingness; it's about creating a clearing. It's opening up an emotionally clutter-free space and**

allowing ourselves to feel and think and dream and question." ~ Brené Brown.

This is when I began to look inside myself instead of blaming others. I changed my anger and judgments to compassion. That's when the real story began to unfold. The abrupt turn in my thoughts changed my entire story. I would begin my story showing the reader what it felt like as a child who didn't understand how being an empath affected my life. As a child, I regulated my body by being outside, swimming, and playing. I held onto words inside my body. It was the way I was born and I had to accept who I was instead of running or blaming. It was time to stop blaming my mother and discover **who I am, a highly sensitive person.**

"**When I change the way I look at things, the things I look at change.**" ~ Wayne Dyer

---

### Mindfulness or Mindfullness?

- I am mindful when I am in the moment.
- I am mind**full** when I am thinking about the past or the future.
- I am mindful when I pay attention to my surroundings - sights, sounds, and feelings.
- I am mind**full** when I am thinking about too many things.
- I am mindful when I let go and let God.
- I am mindful when I observe instead of judge. Nothing is good nor bad. It just is.

---

**Questions to Ponder:**

- What, in your research, has given you new insight or a whole different way to look at things? Do you want to share these details with your readers?
- What do you know now that you didn't know when you began your writing journey?
- What information will the reader need in order to understand the new information?
- What have you learned from your research or new insight that you will use when editing your writing?
- Do you need to go back to the research phase to learn more about this new information?
- What is the main message you want your reader to take away?
- To connect with your body, put your hand over your heart, take a few deep breaths. How do you feel about this?
- How do you connect to your subconscious using mindfulness practices?

**"Your message is the moral of your story. And there are people waiting to hear it. A story left unsaid is the saddest story of them all. Share yours now." ~ Rebecca Campbell**

## My Self Publishing Journey

It's important to have photos done professionally if you choose the path to publishing. You will need them for your website, blog, book and any social media that you use.

I hire a friend to do a photo shoot for the book and my website. We were going to a few different spots for the scenery. As we walk by a house toward the fence, I look up at the house and see the numbers **1188.** *Was this a sign? I had walked by that house several times and never once noticed those numbers. It was a house that had accumulated so much junk on the porch, the exterior and in the field next to it, that the distraction of the "stuff" was so overwhelming that I never saw the numbers. I was clearing away the clutter in my life to see things more clearly- that's why I could see the sign. Those were my repeating numbers which I feel are signs from my Angels- **11 and 88**- Signs to me that the photo shoot was a necessary part of writing this book.*

*"**Angel number 11 is a message from the angels concerning your soul mission or greater life purpose. When the angels send you messages containing Master Number 11 they are sending you inspiration and encouragement to develop your abilities in ways that will help all of humanity.**" retrieved from, https://thesecretofthetarot.com/ angel-number-11/*

*And the number 8 was my nephew, Tyler's favorite number. I was walking on the new shiny path. Although the path was shiny and new, I had angels walking with me as I wrote my first book.*

I tried to shut off the negative voice inside my head saying that having a photo shoot was a dumb idea. Seeing those numbers immediately changed my thinking to positive thoughts. It went something like this, *"Sam (my photographer) knows me so well that these pictures are going to be amazing. How lucky am I that she is in my life? Nobody else would be able to capture "ME" in these photos. She knows me and is so excited about this project. Enjoy it. Love myself as she takes my picture. I know that I am more than my physical body. She will see inside my soul when she takes my picture. Other people will see my soul too. When they read the book, it will help them to be in touch with their soul, too."* I am uplifted by my thoughts and I begin to enjoy the photo shoot.

**Book Release Date**

With self publishing companies, it's difficult to determine the exact date of release and when it will be available for purchase. With a traditional publisher, it takes longer (at least 12-18 months) and you can pre-order the books.

When my book was available on Amazon, I was not notified. I began watching every day. One day - there it was! I overnight shipped it and it arrived the next day. I had my husband videotape me opening my book and posted it on social media. It was approximately nine months since I first put pen to paper and began my writing journey.

At Balboa, when the book goes live (meaning it is available for purchase), my contacts at Balboa change from production to a Marketing and Editorial Consultant. *You'll never believe what happened during the first phone call! As the people at Balboa will say, "There are no coincidences at Balboa or Hay House. The universe will give plenty of signs."*

*After speaking with my Marketing and Editorial Consultant for over an hour about my book, I said, "I'm sorry. I didn't catch your name." She responds, "DeeAnna." This was my Mother's name!!! - spelled a little differently, but at the time I did not know this! If I was looking for my Mother's approval - I think I got it!*

*DeeAnna then helped me plan how to get my book out to the world. She talked to me about my Platform (my online presence through social media, website, etc) and what I was planning on doing for outreach. She suggested different services from Balboa and guided me in the right direction. She calls and checks in to see where I am with marketing my book.*

*DeeAnna even told me her dime story! She told me about hiking a mountain with her boyfriend and along the hike she found two dimes. She said she immediately thought of me and thought the dimes were like bread crumbs up the mountain. Then, when she got to the top, her boyfriend proposed to her! She said the dimes made it even more special!*

"To be free, to truly experience life, you must come out. You have to let go and pass through the cleansing process that frees you from your psyche." ~ Michael A. Singer

# Chapter Seven: Planned or Unplanned?

*"Who is 'turning the knobs'? To make everything happen."*
*~James H. Palmer*

**"The day unfolds and the mind doesn't say anything. You simply interact with the day with a peaceful, fully inspired heart. " ~ Michael A. Singer**

I like to plan my day, my life, my everything. When I decide I want to do something, it's like my body thinks I'm already there, doing it instead of being present in the moment. It's hard for me to let life happen and enjoy it as it comes. But, when I do, miracles happen!

While writing my first book, my husband and I are traveling from Vermont to Delaware to visit friends. We randomly pull into a rest stop along our way. I am driving and have lots and lots of choices of where to park. I almost park in one spot, then decide at the last second to park in a different space. My husband looks up and notices a man standing next to his car- directly in front of us. He says, "I think that is Roger". We haven't seen him in years. As we get out of the car, my husband says, "Hey there!"

Our friend, Roger, is moving to live with his son. *Was I guided to park in that particular spot? There are several other rest areas we could have stopped at. There are 100's if not 1,000's of people at this particular* *rest area and we park **directly next to someone we know from Vermont?** What are the chances? God brought us together for one last good bye. Most likely we will never see him again in person. I am always amazed at how the universe works- sort of like my Dad suggests, "Who is 'turning the knobs'? To make everything happen."*

Our psyche likes to feel safe. We feel safe when we plan and try to control what is going to happen. It is a constant battle inside. When things don't go as planned, it can be easy to feel upset or emotional. I lived like this for a long time. Writing my first book was most definitely not something I planned and I wouldn't be able to control what happened after it was published. I had to learn to trust that this unplanned surprise in my life was planned by something greater than me.

### October 13, 2018

I was in a store where a TV was on. I am not sure what the show was as I couldn't actually see the TV. *They were about to take a commercial break and all I heard was, **"And, when we get back, we will learn how one single coin can change your life."** Ha! A sign? No doubt! I left the store so I have no idea what it was all about, but I knew that **one single coin** had seriously changed my life! Was the unplanned coin a part of a bigger plan?*

### November 16, 2018

I am working from home on a snow day and an email comes through about a class I will be teaching to adults in the Southern New Hampshire University Master's program, the same program I went through to get my Master's degree. *The class is called "Dimensions in Curriculum and Management" but there isn't room for the entire title. All that shows up is, "(name of person) has invited you to join Dime".*

### December 23, 2018

Today is my Mom's birthday. I am baking for Christmas and go to the store to get a few things. The store is very busy and has all the registers open. I get in line. The woman in front of me bends over to pick something up. She says really loudly, almost like she is making a big announcement to everyone in the store, *"I just found a DIME!!! I found one yesterday too!" I thought she had won the lottery; she was so excited! I look at her and say, "That is very interesting because I am writing a book called Dimes from Heaven and am about to send it to the publisher!"* She looks at her arms and says, "Oh my, I have such goosebumps right now. I don't understand. Are the Spirits trying to contact me?" I laugh and remind her that spirits are not scary like ghosts you might see in the movies. She asks me for my name and really wants to read my book. Thank you Pat McAllister! I hope you get to read my book someday!

**January 8, 2019**

*My son is in a Vermont Public Service TV commercial about being safe when driving near plow trucks. The series is called, "Don't Crowd the Plow" and is sponsored by the Vermont Agency of Transportation. The first quote on one video says, "These trucks cannot stop on a dime." My father is getting pretty clever now!*

**Synchronicities seemed to be taking over my life.**

**"What is Synchronicity? The term is coined by Carl Jung to express a concept that belongs to him:** *the acausal connection of two or more psychic and physical phenomena." ~retrieved from https://www.carl-jung.net/synchronicity.html*

**Planned vs Unplanned**
- I planned to publish my book.
- The universe understands the plan more than I do.
- I could plan what the book would look like.
- I wouldn't be able to plan for what would happen after my story was shared.
- Sometimes when we let go of the plan, the unplanned is so much better!

**Questions to Ponder:**

- Have you discovered your voice? Your own, unique style of writing?
- How will your story inspire others?
- Has the reader felt inspired through your story?
- Discover your WHY. Why do you want to write? What is pushing you to do this? Research Simon Sinek if you need help discovering your why.
- Be you and be proud of it.
- Address any lingering fears that might be lurking around in the background. Bring them to the surface and face them.

**"You don't need to pretend or prove that you have it together, rather, just share what you have figured out so far. We are all in this school of life together. There is no final destination, no end point, just increased consciousness and a deeper understanding." ~** Rebecca Campbell

### My Self Publishing Journey

There is so much that needs to go into the business aspect of writing a book. I had my website designed by a professional and then I needed some physical printing completed: things like business cards, bookmarks, fliers for my book launch and a poster to display for events. I asked around for advise on options and had at least five different businesses to choose from. I chose a place in a town about forty five minutes away to have my business cards printed. I stop by to pick up the cards. As I am chatting with the owner and sale person, they ask about my book, *"Is it something about dimes?"* I reply with a year- it's a pretty cool story. **Then they proceed to tell me that they have a DIME glued to their floor of the office. For REAL!** It was put there as a joke to a previous employee. The employee always had holes in his pockets so his change was constantly falling on the floor. They thought it would be funny to glue a dime to the floor to see if he would try to pick it up! **Out of all the places I could have chosen to print my business cards, I chose the place that had a dime glued to the floor!** *Seriously?!?*

Becoming an author is very similar to starting a business. For me, I enjoyed the writing part of creating a book. The business part used a different part of my brain. I read the book *Platform Get Noticed in a Busy World* by Michael Hyatt. In this book are all of the ins and outs, do's and don't's that a person would need in order to "get noticed". Along with the website and the materials being printed, I needed a game plan where to market my book. I would do a mixture of in-person events and online targeting. Read the book for the nitty-gritty details!

"**Intuition is not a single way of knowing - it's our ability to hold space for uncertainty and our willingness to trust the many ways we've developed knowledge and insight, including instinct, experience, faith and reason.**" ~ Brené Brown

# Chapter Eight:  Inside or Outside?

"We exist largely in theta brainwaves state for our first six to seven years of life, absorbing the world like a sponge and forming beliefs about self, others, and the world." ~ Nikki Gresham-Record

Writing Prompt- "Yes, I lied." Here is my response:

For sure. Without a doubt. I didn't know how to speak the truth. I didn't think anyone would believe me. I thought people would be angry if they heard the truth.

I didn't think it was safe to say it out loud. I thought that people weren't ready to hear it. I thought if I lied, then they would believe the lie. But, in truth, they all knew the truth. They could not only feel it but they could see it in my eyes. They knew I was lying even though I didn't want them to know.

It was the elephant in the room that I wasn't ready to talk about. It would mean I would have to face the truth.

*How would I ever be able to do that? What would help me be able to face it?* I can't believe this is happening. Especially now, of all the times in my life. *Why couldn't it happen next week, after I have been able to talk about it and accept it?*

I can't lie. I don't know how to do it. Internally, I am sick and my body listens to everything my mind thinks. *Why did I ever think I would be able to do this?*

I couldn't do it even when I tried. I ended up blurting the truth and apologizing. Lying is not something I can do. I think because it hurts so much when it happens to me. It cuts into my heart and I can't seem to cut into someone else's heart. It's not how I am built. It isn't inside me to do that.

Do you see how much changed in that short writing? This is an example of taking a topic and journaling on it for about 7-10 minutes. When I started writing, I wasn't sure where my writing would take me. This is the power of writing by hand, without worrying about a polished final draft. I let go of the outcome and enjoyed the writing process.

I wrote this at a weekend writing retreat led by Joni B. Cole, a Vermont author and professor of writing (https://www.jonibcole.com/). I learned several things that weekend that helped me in my writing.

There is a rhythm to the writing I like to do. I like to share stories. She explained that we first show the reader something, tell more about it and then reflect. The "back story" means so much more when you have a "front" story. Writers show emotions with scenes. There is a "Rule of 3". 1. Bring it up 2. Repeat it 3. Resonate the why- the symbolism. Most people remember some of the stories in *Dimes from Heaven.* One of the best examples of this was regarding my favorite pair of boots that I didn't take care of (front story). I compared these to relationships in my life (back story-reflection). By not taking care of my boots, they were ruined. I couldn't go back in time to care for them. Relationships can be like that. I don't get to go back in time and re-do it. I can only change my actions from now on. The boots represented mistakes I made in my life.

Most of my internal messages about life were buried within me from years of my insides not matching my outside world. I stopped listening to my gut when I was young because people around me told me my gut wasn't right. When people told me lies, I was told to believe them, even though inside I felt something different. I learned to shut off and disconnect from my body and I didn't know how to listen anymore. I had to relearn this and it took a long time!

I learned from a young age to be alert for danger. I have always had extreme anxiety and I wasn't aware of it. I learned that it was super important to listen carefully because if I didn't, there might be consequences. If I missed a cue like, "Clean up your room," I might be reminded again in a harsher tone of voice. Maybe not screaming, but in my mind it felt like I should be ashamed of myself for not listening the first time. I learned to read body language. Any little fluctuation in someone's eyes, mouth or facial expression could mean serious danger to me. By looking at the outside (their slight body movements), I thought I knew what was happening on the inside.

Often times, we make stories in our heads and add to them to make them great. Brene Brown calls these "Shitty first drafts." Some aspects may be true and whatever we tell ourselves we seem to believe. But, the story is only true based on our perspective and it is our psyche (subconscious) talking to us. Someone else may believe something totally different. At the beginning of *Dimes from Heaven*, I put in a disclaimer, "I have tried to recreate events, locales and conversations from my memories of them. These memories are from my perspective only. Others may or may not remember them as I do."

I re-read parts about my Mom or Dad and the passages didn't "sit right" in my gut. Things like "My mother was insecure" changed to "I sensed my mother might be insecure" or "*Was my mother insecure?*" I took ownership of the feelings and stated everything from my point of view. *I was only looking into the "windows" of my mother.*

*I really couldn't tell how she felt inside and I had no business writing it as a fact. I sorted through the "lies" I was telling myself in order to protect my ego. This was Spirit guiding me, nudging me to help myself heal with my words. I was facing my truth even though it didn't feel good inside. I wasn't going to listen to the voice inside my head anymore.*

### August 5, 2018

We stop off at a lake on our way home from camping. My husband was kayaking and I was on my paddle board. We are enjoying the day and I am swimming near my paddle board. A dragonfly lands on my paddle board. I remember when I was a kid I would always brush them away because I was scared of them. As an adult, I know that some people view them as a sign from a loved one. *I stare at the dragonfly on my paddle board and in my head ask, "Who are you?" This one felt new and different. I decide that I think too much and let it go.*

We get back to the boat launch, load up and head home. I decide to check Facebook and the first status I see is a post from one of my husband's cousins. *One of their beloved cousins transitioned to spirit after battling brain cancer for a year and a half. I begin to cry. I know that the dragonfly was David in his new spirit form.*

I first started studying Louise Hay in 1996 and Brian Weiss in 2008. When I talked with people about certain things in life, I began pointing them to books. I'll never forget one woman saying to me, "You always have a good book to mention about everything. I wish I had that much time to read!" I realized that *Dimes from Heaven* was actually like my thesis about life. I was summarizing a bunch of different authors I had read over the years and how their work related to my life. I discovered I was actually writing a memoir. *But, it wasn't a regular memoir; I learned I was writing a **teaching memoir.***

I stop by the library at one of the schools where I work. I am chatting with the librarian about the new books for kids. I explain how I used to read a lot of the young adult books when I was teaching 5th and 6th grade, but now I am enjoying reading other books. . She says she tries to keep up on the latest kid books too. I share that my favorite books are based on true stories. She replies, "Ooooooo, I **LOVE** memoirs!" I think, *"Ooooooo, maybe you'll **LOVE** my memoir!!" I feel tingles throughout my entire body as I imagine all the people who would read my book.*

**Inside or Outside?**
- I felt uncomfortable on the inside when I tried to blame things on the outside.
- I had to look inside to connect to my true self.
- I had to understand that nothing on the outside would be able to hurt me.
- I understood that due to my sensitive nature, I might misread body cues. I wouldn't be able to tell what someone was thinking on the inside by looking at the outside of their physical body.
- I had to feel God on the inside.
- I had to realize that what I felt on the inside would help me attract things on the outside.

## Questions to Ponder:

- What do you feel on the inside?

- What signs are you seeing on the outside?
- How will the outside help you inside?
- What inside of you needs to be healed?

"When you follow what you love, the Universe will pick up on your expanded feelings and send you more things to match your newly found expansion." ~ Rebecca Campbell

## My Self-Publishing Journey

Because I was writing a memoir with real people and real lives, I needed to make sure that everyone was okay with the material I was writing about. It didn't make sense to me to change the names of people to protect them. At times, this might be valuable for non-fiction. I decided to have people read over the manuscript to make sure they were okay with what I wrote.

As part of my Balboa publishing package, their editors would also look for content in which they thought either someone might get upset about or laws about using other people's materials. I learned that it is okay to quote a few sentences here or there from another author, but not too much. Whole pages of content were not allowed. Songs and poems are also a place where you need the writer's permission to use their content. Originally, I had some of the words to songs in my writing but learned that was not something I could use in my book.

Although I wrote my material inside during the quiet moments of solitude, it was now time to share my story with the outside world.

"We don't discover our soul calling, we uncover it by following the trail of things that light us up and then lose ourselves in the doing." ~ Rebecca Campbell

## Chapter Nine: Comfortable or Uncomfortable?

"I didn't *want* to think about stuff that made me uncomfortable. And I certainly didn't want to feel any of it." ~Seane Corn

When writing, I had some of the worst anxiety EVER! Sharing my story was scary! It made me very uncomfortable on a physical level. My body didn't like me sharing "inside" information. *How would I ever dare to share my story?* The signs kept coming that this "project" was worth it! As a Southern New Hampshire University student told me, "I had to learn to be comfortable with being uncomfortable." *I seriously didn't like the sound of that! Luckily, the universe was supporting me every step of the way.*

One of the books Reid Tracy recommended in the Hay House Writer's workshop was Choose Yourself, Be Happy, Make Millions, Live the Dream by James Altucher. James references dimes throughout his entire book. *First sentence of the book, "I don't need to make a dime off of this book." For real? I guess I am reading the book I am meant to read! Some of the other sentences throughout his book are: "I never raised a dime for that business." "But more important is to build relationships than to kill everyone and take every last dime in a negotiation." "At the drop of a dime, I would show up for dinner wherever and whenever he asked me to." "Ideas are a dime a dozen." Thank you, James Altucher - I think I'll choose myself!*

This book gave me the strength to accept myself as an empath and highly sensitive person. I had to accept myself first and then own my story. I had to believe that sharing my story about being an empath would help others. I began to revise by looking at my life through the lens of being an empath.

I believe every high school student should read *Choose Yourself Be Happy, Make Millions, Live the Dream*. In this book, James explains that not everyone has to go to college and follow that path. We all have options and we should choose what we are passionate about. It really made me think about my choices for my career. Did I have to stay in the same career path that I had decided when I was seventeen years old or was there something more for me to do in this lifetime? How would I ever leave the job that provided me with security and safety? How would I step into the unknown and be able to trust that this was what I was supposed to do? One step at a time...One day at a time...

Now that I had discovered I was an empath, I had to integrate that into my story. This one key piece of information transformed my entire viewpoint. Admitting this to the world would be difficult but I felt the need to share this information. *I believed by admitting this, it would help others. Some people might be able to relate and some would not. I felt that by having the words to explain how I felt, it helped me accept myself and understand I wasn't alone.*

**"To end suffering, you must first realize that your psyche is not okay. You must then acknowledge that it does not have to be that way. It can be healthy...You don't have to constantly be mulling over what you said or what this person thinks of you." ~ Michael A. Singer**

I didn't want to teach about being an empath in the middle of my story. I was trying to think of a way for the reader to learn but not be preachy. That's when I decided to explain further in Dimes From Heaven, Section Two is called Who am I and Why am I like This? It would give the reader information about how being an empath affects my everyday life. It would also explain tools and strategies for highly sensitive people or empaths.

I am going to be totally honest about using the quotes throughout my book. They were my security blanket. I worried about people thinking I was making this stuff up. I thought that if I quoted other authors talking about our connection to heaven, it would help make my story valid. I also hoped that the reader might want to read more about the topics. I secretly wanted people to be curious about Brené Brown, Judith Orloff, or other authors. I was planting seeds of information to get the readers curious. Even if they didn't, they were getting some of the main topics throughout my memoir!

I imagined different "threads" of thought throughout my book and asked myself questions like the following:

- Where does the idea of an empath begin and where does it go?
- How will the reader understand about past lives?
- What will the reader learn about food choices?
- How will I address the non-believer? That's where the chapter starts with "The living can't speak to the dead." ~ Mitch Albom and ends with "You're not a jack-ass whisperer." ~ Scott Straten.
- How will I incorporate the suspense of the dimes? Leading up to finding the dimes? Make sure to sprinkle a little hint in each chapter!
- How could I use italicized writing to put emphasis on some things?
- How would I transition the reader when I jumped from Florida and then back to the dime story?

By asking myself questions, I was able to integrate my ideas better.

Messages can come from anywhere. Here are a few more that I felt were signs during my writing journey.

**July 5, 2018**

While waiting to get an oil change on my car, the TV is playing a news show about "Veterans Helping Veterans". The thought behind the program is to change the PTSD negative thinking to be more positive thoughts about growth and change. They explain that we hold our emotions in our cells and our body remembers. If you fail to deal with your feelings, then they will get stuck inside your body. It's important to rewrite the story you are telling yourself inside your head.

*Wait, is that a coin around his wife's neck? Could it be? I'll have to check again after the commercial.*

I watch more of the segment, not quite able to hear everything. I'm reading the book, The First Phone Call from Heaven by Mitch Albom. In the book, it is talking about how Alexander Graham Bell almost didn't go to the convention where his phone was being displayed. He jumped on the train at the last minute because of love. His wife didn't want to be away from him. That moment in time would change history. The telephone would become a way to communicate with people. This didn't have anything to do with the Vet's story, but a quick segment came on about how to make homemade speakers for your cell phone-out of two paper cups and a piece of cardboard! How would that ever work? Ha! Was this a sign? You bet! I was writing about the "new" spirit communication system I had explained to my father. I described how the spirit communication system was like a telephone - a new way to communicate with people in Heaven.

I might not have watched the segment if the woman's necklace hadn't caught my eye. *In another 10 years, would people be talking about how the spirit connection system works like a telephone? How everyone would have the ability to access it as easily as a cell phone? I felt the positivity of the news article about changing trauma into something positive in my bones. Imagine if all news was only positive? Would everyone be happier? 10 years ago we would never have imagined talking to someone on top of a mountain with a little black box (a cell phone). Will we be able to phone Heaven easily in another 10 years?*

*The next day, I write all morning and then take a break to enjoy the sunshine and pick apples. On my way home, I am thinking of the last few chapters and some things I want to add. As I am about to go up my driveway on my way home, I look at the time. 11:55 and the temperature on the car thermometer is 55. Guess my angels are telling me it is time to work on my book!*

When I get home there is a small snake next to my front step. I decide to look up the meaning of snake in the Animal Spirit Guides book by Steven Farmer to see what sign the snake means.

**"You're about to go through some significant personal changes, so intense and dramatic that an old self will metaphorically die as a new self emerges. You're going to feel a surge of energy that will sharpen your senses, alert your mental faculties, and open up new channels of awareness. You're about to resolve a long-standing issue, one that has required a great deal of your attention, by seeing things in a new light. It would be a good time for you to start doing either tantric or kundalini yoga. You'll experience a dramatic and unexpected physical or emotional healing very soon, coming from an unexpected source." ~ Steven Farmer**

This was shortly after I had gone back to the parts about my Mom and made sure that I wrote that this was how I "felt", not trying to guess what her internal feelings were. **Sentences like, "My Mom was insecure" turned into "I sensed that my Mom was insecure."** *I had no idea what was happening within my mother and made sure to mention how I felt instead. I had spent a lot of years judging my mother because it was easier than admitting I was different than others. At times, I didn't want this gift of being an empath. I had to learn to accept the gift and learn how to deal with the challenges. I was most definitely going through a huge transformation!*

*A lot of people loved my Mom and I wanted to make sure that I took responsibility for my feelings. She was a wonderful person who enjoyed people.*

### Comfortable vs Uncomfortable

- I was comfortable in my life as an educator.
- I was uncomfortable thinking about a new career in writing. I wouldn't be able to plan what would happen.
- I was comfortable with blaming and judging other people. By judging them, I realized, I also judged myself and this is what caused some of my anxiety!
- I was uncomfortable looking within myself for the answers.
- I was comfortable hiding my story.
- I was uncomfortable sharing my belief in God and being an empath.
- I had to learn to be comfortable being uncomfortable because I knew that my soul was growing through a process of self-acceptance.

"Contentment arrives when our wholeness comes from within. If we define ourselves by how much money we make, how many friends we have, or how many things we own, we can never be satisfied. There's never enough out there to fill the emptiness inside because what we're actually lacking is a sense of our own goodness, a sense that yes, we *are* enough." ~ Seane Corn

### Questions to Ponder:

- Have you integrated your main message with all of your smaller messages?
- How does your writing flow?
- Do you have a clear beginning, middle and end?
- What voice makes the most sense?
- Is your voice consistent throughout the entire book?
- Who have you asked to read your book and give you feedback?
- Are you using the feedback to make your writing better?
- Do your readers understand the main messages?
- What messages from the universe did you integrate into your book?

- Is there more information you need? Do you need to go back to the research phase?
- Quiet your mind and be open to the answer coming from Spirit or your intuition.

"The world is filled with people who, no matter what you do, will point blank not like you. But it is filled with those who will love you fiercely. They are your people. You are not for everyone and that's OK. Talk to the people who can hear you." ~ Rebecca Campbell

## My Self Publishing Journey THE FINAL TOUCHES
### November 21, 2018

*I am filing my bills and receipts. I pick up a receipt from one of the herbal supplements I purchased to help me heal. Normally, I would just file the receipt but I decide to look at the receipt and notice the address for the company includes* **Palmer St**. *Palmer is my maiden name!*

Some other parts to a book that you might want to think about are:

- **Note from the author** - Do you have something to say to the reader before they begin reading?
- **Foreword** - Is there someone who would be willing to write this for you? Someone who knows you and is connected to the topic you are writing about.
- **Resources** - If you use any quotes, make sure to include the books, websites, etc. in your resources/bibliography.
- **Cover** - Hire a professional to do your cover. Some publishing companies will help you with this.
- **Epilogue** - Does the reader need to know something else that will help them understand the story? Something that might be after the main story?

I call the photographer who did my Senior photos and wedding pictures. He has lots of pictures of Elmore Mountain, where I found one of the first dimes from my Dad. When I asked him for a photo, he says most of his photos are of sunsets. If I want a daytime photo of the mountain, I should call someone else. I refuse; explaining that I want him to be a part of my book. He took photos of my wedding and I want him, not some other photographer. He thinks and then says, "Well, is your book Spiritual at all?" *Huh? Is he like the minister on the mountain - asking me if I have Faith?* "Oh my Gosh! Yes - my book is very spiritual! What are you thinking?" I ask. He responds, "*I have the perfect picture for you. I just have to find it...*" Months later, after digging through ten or more hard drives, he would send me the photo that is on the front cover. It was the perfect picture for my book cover.

**What makes a good title?**

Write down several titles while writing and don't worry about the final choice until the very end. Choose several titles and ask friends or other writers which ones make them curious about your book.

The entire time that I was writing, my book was called "More Than a Dime." I couldn't see it any other way. Then, I realized that the reader wouldn't understand what the book was about if it had that title. My dimes were from my father, who was in the spirit world or Heaven. The reader needed to know this from the start.

The subtitle gives the reader more information and may be longer than the title. After I discovered I was an empath, I knew this had to be a part of the subtitle. I wanted people to learn what the word meant. It was also the most scary part because even if people didn't read my book, I was admitting that I was different! I wouldn't "fit in" but I would belong! It wasn't until one of the last edits where I was sitting with my friend, Tracy, that the final title was born. While discussing my writing, she said, "I LOVE the part where you say 'the beginning of the word coincidence is **coin.**" We both say "that's the second part of the title!" at the same time! It was magical and we both got goosebumps!

A new title was born. It changed from *Dimes From Heaven How a Few Dimes From Heaven Helped Me Discover My Life as an Empath* to *Dimes From Heaven How Coins and Coincidences helped Me Discover My Life as an Empath*. It was the final step I needed before sending my manuscript to the editor!

**Online Presence- Building my Platform**

Because I was a public educator writing a spiritual based book, I was VERY uncomfortable about sharing. I began my author Facebook page right before my book was released. Honestly, it was so frightening for me! I did two free drawings to try to get people to share, like, and comment on a post on Facebook. Within the first few weeks, I had almost 400 likes to my page. Then it began to slow down. Facebook was the platform I was most comfortable with and where I spent most of my time. Putting myself "out there" in the world was risky and scary, but I had faith that it was important for me to share.

It is incredible how you can target an audience in a Facebook Advertisement. From interests, to age, or location, your sponsored ad will bring in the audience you are looking for.

I named everything Monica L. Morrissey. My Facebook, Instagram, email and website would all match. The reader would just type in monicalmorrissey.com and instantly they would be able to find me. At first, I thought I would brand my sites with dimesfromheaven.com, but I learned that my followers would be following me, not just my first book. Dimes From Heaven would be my first book, but what about after that? Was this book going to be the end? Or, was it actually just the beginning of my new adventure? Would every book, blog, post, etc always be about Dimes? Maybe, maybe not. I had to leave that door open by naming everything with my name.

I immediately loved connecting with my readers about my book! It filled up the cup of love inside me. I imagined my book had wings and the love inside helped make it fly all over the world. It was up to me to give it a little push here and there.

I imagined that every book I sold or gave away, it produced a sale of at least ten more books. "What is the the way most people find out about a good book? One that your friends or family recommends!" ~ Reid Tracy, CEO of Hay House. One by one, I was producing more love and happiness in the world. Some would choose to read it and some would not be ready to read it. It wasn't up to me to decide- I let go of the outcome and knew inside that the book would continue each and every day to make a difference.

Nick Ortnor (The Tapping Solution by Hay House Publishers) says that if you don't have a one star review, not enough people have read your book. I braced myself for the negative feedback. It came sooner than I suspected and from people I didn't expect. Some of my good friends never said a word about my book when it was first released. *Did they know about my book? Why wouldn't they support me? Aren't we supposed to encourage our friends to follow their dreams?* It was confusing for sure! Then, acquaintances contacted me telling me how much my book changed their life! While one person said, "There's a lot about God in it. It surprised me. I didn't know you were so religious," the next person said, "I loved how you talked about spirituality not having to be about religion." A song came on the radio about this time. It was "Jesus Freak". I asked the first person if she read where I explain about the difference between Spirit and Religion. She did but I felt she was still stuck in the subconscious programming of our society's view of God in a structured religion. I had to learn how to let go of what some people thought about my book.

At times, the publishing world and book stores were overwhelming. *How would I be able to get my book on a book shelf in a bookstore?* I was a lone, self-published author with no help from a publishing company. I decided to go through some back doors to get my book on a shelf.

While on trips to Oregon and Florida in 2019, I got my book on a book-shelf in two used bookstores. I sold my book for $2-$3. I secretly imagined someone finding this gem on the used bookshelf and then telling all their friends about it! This was, of course, after the person at the counter of the used book store had perused it!

No matter if you are a self-published or a traditional published author, marketing is your responsibility. I imagined my book sprinkled all over the world like confetti. There would be one sprinkle that turned into many sprinkles. It was one book at a time!

Locally, I posted on Facebook that I had books if anyone wanted a signed copy. I loved hand delivering them, especially to people I hadn't seen in years. Online, I reached out to other self-published authors. I read their books and, in return, they read mine. I was slowly gaining momentum as a published author.

I was initially shocked when Balboa told me the price of my book would be $32.99. This was strictly based on word count, color pictures, and the layout. I cringed. Would people really pay that much for a book? *I had to believe they would.*

I worked with local bookstores to try to get my book on their book shelves. It was an interesting experience as a first time, self-published author. I had purchased a lot of books at bookstores throughout the years and I walked in naively thinking that they would support authors, especially a local author! Their words said they wanted to support me, but some of their actions didn't feel supportive.

There is most definitely an interesting dynamic with the internet world of Amazon and local, Indie bookstores. Amazon was out of my control as far as the price for my book. The price would change daily at times and the lowest it went was about $24.00. My eBook was originally priced at $9.99 but that also fluctuated. I advertised a mixture of ideas of where people could get my book. If people were local, please go to the local bookstore. But, I was meeting people from all around the world! I had a person in Australia want my book but it was going to cost $60 just to ship it! The e-book would be a way to reach people on the other side of the world.

I most definitely listened to the voice inside at first and reacted with anger and frustration. Then, I dug a little deeper into the publishing world. I was "different" than a "real" author because I "self-published". I felt like I was a second class citizen. I wondered about this a lot. I began to realize that the publishing world was really controlling what we, as Americans, read. I heard stories from Hay House authors that they were turned down by seventeen different publishing companies! *What was going on in the publishing world that I didn't know or understand?* I realized that book store owners want to make sure their inventory is going to sell. I believe they stock famous authors and books that get a lot of attention. This is how the publishing companies control what we read and who has a voice to share their story. I wondered where I fit into this puzzle. I was not famous and I didn't have a traditional publishing company to support my work.

This is how the nitty gritty works when you are an unknown, first time, self-published author eager to get your book on a bookshelf. My publishing company would sell me my book at a discounted rate, depending on how many books I bought. Most of the time, I purchased 100 books at 60% of the full price. All publishers are different - this was the rate I was given for the number of books I was able to purchase at one time. Then, I would ask a bookstore to stock my book. They would sell my book on consignment. The split? They would give me 60% and they would keep 40%. Basically, I would make nothing. I don't get my royalties on books that I purchase directly from my publishing company. I chose to do this and believe that it was worth it. I felt I had a bigger purpose. I wanted to share my book with the world! If this was what I had to do, then I was willing to do it.

On the other hand, a larger bookstore like Barnes and Noble was different. I walked into our Vermont based Barnes and Noble and explained that I was a Vermont author. I asked if they would be willing to stock my book on their shelf. They immediately agreed and ordered my book on the spot. They placed it in a key location near the register and for months, whenever I stopped by to check, if the book had sold, they would happily order another. I realized that with as many books as they had on their shelves, it was up to me to make sure that they restocked my book.

Amazon has most definitely opened up the world to a self-published author like myself. I met all kinds of other writers through online Facebook Writing groups - mostly through Hay House. I met people from all over the world who read my book and I read their book.

One author I met even had a story about a dime in her book!

**"I have experienced some very profound events that are signs from Rick...He sends me dimes to remind me that with time all will be**

**well. Time on a dime." ~ Lisa Marie Runfola from her book A Limit-less Life in a Powerless World**

I felt that although we want to support our local businesses, it would be very difficult for me to continue the path of approaching every single bookstore - *all over the world?!?* - to get my book on shelves. It just wasn't possible. I would need to use Amazon. I wouldn't be able to solve the digital world problem of purchasing vs. supporting local businesses. I was on a mission to share my book and the internet allowed me to do that.

I learned that publishing companies have controlled what we have been reading for years. I had read Brendan Bouchard's book The Golden Ticket. I loved the book! The character was doing a life review and then realized that we only get one ticket for our life. We have to use it properly because there isn't another one. It seriously changed my life and now I appreciate each and every day. But, the interesting thing that I learned while writing my book? Seventeen publishers said, "No" to Brendan's book proposal. He finally found a publisher that would publish his book. Imagine if he had given up? I never would have read his book and I never would have thought about life in a very different way. I know publishers most likely get a lot of book proposals for books, but it is time for every-one to have a voice and be able to write their own book without relying on approval from big publishing companies.

Through Balboa Publishing, I hired a Publicist. They knew more about how to get my book to the places it needed to get to in order to be noticed by the book world. This was not a world that I was familiar with. They knew where to send the press release and how to get my book noticed. This process can be at anytime after the book is released. For me, I waited about 4 months after my book was released. I had some Amazon reviews and the book was gaining momentum. This process would give it a whole new wave of sales! Through this publicist, I was able to get media cover-age all over the United States and they even secured some interviews for me!

## Book Launch Party

I began studying about book launch parties. (check out https://www.au-thorlearningcenter.com/) In my head, this coincided with the book release, but that wasn't the case. Book launches can be big parties - almost like a birthday party - or quiet, intimate book signings at a local book store.

When I began to plan my book launch party, I actually began with questions like, "Why did I want people to read my book?" The answer to the question guided me in my planning. I wanted people to be happier, learn to care for themselves in a different way and I wanted people to understand that Heaven wasn't as far away as they thought.

The plan began to unfold. I would ask the many healers in the area to provide a sample treatment for 1 hour, paying them with a free book. Then the author of the Foreword would speak. A local documentary about the Adverse Childhood Experience (ACE) study would also be shown, highlighting how emotions affect our physical health- my most passionate subject! Kim Pierce was following her soul's calling and created a Vermont based film called, "The Faces of Aces". It would highlight her work at the local health center to help her patients understand the connection of emotions to their physical health. She was changing the world with sharing her passion!

We planned it for a Sunday afternoon. I worked with the local bookstore so that people would be able to purchase books through them. We gave away door prizes and had dime necklaces and dime jars for sale. It was a sunny afternoon and I had a team who helped me.

We started with an hour of mingling and people were able to have acupuncture, massage therapy, sound therapy, Reiki, essential oils and much more! People tried alternative ways to heal and won gift certificates to continue that work. I heard many stories of healing and signs from their loved ones. I spoke at the end and read the first part of this book that you are reading right now. It was truly a magical afternoon.

"Yes, the Universe has got you covered. It wants to support you. We just need to leap in order for it to catch us. Once landed, our life can become one big stream of flow." ~ Rebecca Campbell

## Chapter 10 The End or The Beginning

"There's so much pressure on us to be perfect but that perfect person is just an illusion of our own mind and wanting a perfect life- and comparing our lives to others' so called perfect lives- is a pattern that just creates unnecessary stress and pressure." ~ Anshu Singh

I grew up always worried about money. I realized that I had watched my parents work hard to create a thriving family business. I thought the only answer in life was to go to college, work long hours every day and get as much money as possible. Nobody actually said,

"I want my children to be wealthy, to be better than anyone else, to win at everything they do, to get a good job, to get the best grades, to get into the right schools, to look good to their peers. Yet, this seems to be how they're raising their children." ~ Dr. Wayne Dyer.

This idea was what I internalized at a young age and thought I was supposed to do.

America is obsessed with the thinking mind instead of the spiritual experience in life. We encourage our high school students to think that they need to make a life decision about what they will do for work for the rest of their lives. Most youngsters think that they have to have a traditional job working for a company. I was never encouraged to think of my own idea or create a business idea based on my passion. I was taught to use my rational mind to create a life where I would work in a job to save for my retirement and then I would be able to enjoy my life. I wasn't taught to follow my dreams or my interests.

I realize now that I was experiencing secondary trauma from my teaching job. The symptoms of secondary trauma are: Inability to listen, anger and cynicism, sleeplessness, fear, chronic exhaustion, physical ailments and guilt. I was unable to stop the hamster wheel in my head because I worked all the time and never slowed down. I wasn't taking care of myself. I was busy taking care of everyone else. I had to learn how to slow down and take care of myself. (for more information, read Cheryl Richardson's book Extreme Self-Care) I thought self-care was selfish. It's not. It is so important. I was so busy doing that I was not being.

Nowadays, it seems that we are talking more about finding our own internal strength and valuing each moment we are alive. I can most definitely say that I tried to raise my own children differently. I encouraged them to find out what they wanted to do every day. I wanted them to find a job where they were happy. I knew they would need to be able to make money but I didn't want it to be at the cost of their happiness.

"I want my children to enjoy life, to value themselves, to be risk takers, to become self-reliant, to be free from stress and anxiety, to have peaceful lives, to celebrate their present moments, to experience a lifetime of wellness, to be creative, and above all to fulfill their highest needs and to feel a sense of purpose." ~ Dr. Wayne Dyer

These things are so much more than what money can give us. I can see clearly now that I was meant to be a teacher for most of my life but now I know that writing and sharing my story is helping me take a risk and fulfill a sense of purpose. I thought when I finished writing my first book, I was at the "end" but, in reality, it was only the beginning. The beginning of more writing, more sharing, and helping others write their book!

It's the second to last day of our vacation in Florida. During this week, I've written the first draft for this book. All week I had been thinking about how I had looked furiously in the sand for a dime when writing my first book. I saw lots and lots of seashells, but no dimes.

*My phone rings while sitting on the deck at the condo. It's a loud ring and people by the pool turn to look. I answer it. It's another telemarketer with no voice on the other end. I sit and listen to nothing. I hang up and decide on my attitude. Do I get super angry that I seem to get these type of phone calls daily now? I hang up and look at the time 11:55 on April 11th. Just in case the dime didn't fully give you a message, here are some numbers. There are no mistakes in the universe, not even telemarketers. That phone call helped to send me a message from Spirit, but only if I was willing to see it.*

**"I now pay much closer attention to what shows up for me, and I'm willing to listen carefully to any inclination I might have and act accordingly, even if it leads me into unknown territory. I urge you to do the same." ~ Dr. Wayne Dyer**

My mind remembers the phrase, "That isn't how it works. Faith is believing even when you can't see any proof." I'm also thinking about giving up meat for my health because of the messages from the universe telling me my system was too sensitive to be able to process meat. I again don't want to accept this message, wanting to be "normal" and eat whatever I want. I still think belonging means to fit into society's norms.

"Begin to pay close attention and view every event and every circumstance - in particular, those that result in dramatic shifts - as guidance from this Divine organizing intelligence." ~ Dr. Wayne Dyer

Then, as we are walking back from the beach, out of nowhere, appears a dime in the sand! I say to my husband, as I bend down to pick it up, "Guess what this is?" He responds, "Is it a Liberty Head?" He knows it is a dime, but wouldn't that be a BIG miracle if it was a Liberty Head dime? *It wasn't but my message is clear. I have my answer. "Your system is sensitive and my body feels better by cutting down on my meat intake." I begin to heal even more.*

*I imagine my father grinning yet again. A voice, like the one on the mountain, whispers to me,* **"This is such a fun game! Can we keep playing?"** *I also hear him say,* **"Write that second book. I know you can do it!"**

I look at the year of the dime - **2013.** The year often signals a message. *Any significance? Well, this morning when I opened up my memories on my Timehop APP, a picture of my Dad and my son, Patrick, popped up. It was the family business's 80th year anniversary. The year?* ***2013.***

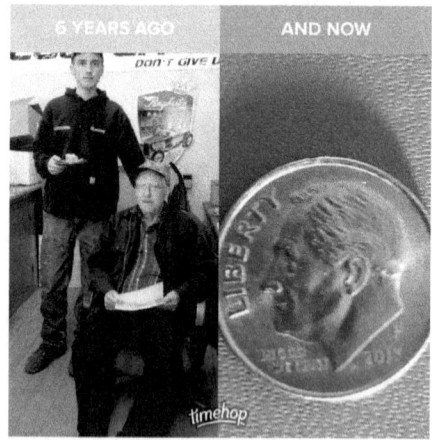

Many people have found dimes since they have heard my story. When they find a dime, they automatically think of me. The same

thing happens when a person shares their signs from heaven - dragon-flies, butterflies, cardinals, and rainbows. I begin to see their signs and think of them. In this way, I feel connected to people and feel a sense of belonging to something bigger than our human journey. These people believe and understand that our souls continue on after we leave our human bodies.

**"There are things working on a different level that are impossible to see, but can be felt...Regardless of whether you had a wonderful childhood or a terrible one, it was the perfect playground for your soul's growth." ~ Rebecca Campbell**

As I work on the manuscript and am excited to publish my second book, three birds hit my window. *Could they feel my excitement?* It wasn't like one hit, then a half hour later another one hits the window. They all hit the window within about 60 seconds. Boom. Boom. Boom. I smile as I know it is some sort of sign. (poor little birdies!) I decide to look up to see what a chickadee represents. "..chickadee symbolizes positivity, cheerful natures, flexibility, courage and social behavior." retrieved from https://dreamingandsleeping.com/chickadee-spirit-animal-symbolism-and-meaning/

I realize I will need all of those characteristics in order to be able to publish my second book.

**"Find someone who believes that he is alone, and convince him that he's not." ~ Dr. Wayn Dyer**

Signs can be anything. Now that I am on this path to accepting my-self, I know that I will most likely explore more about my connection to spirit. This connection is available to anyone. Even you. I encourage you to trust your own intuitive abilities. When you think you see a sign, think in your head, *'Who is this and what is their message?'* Whatever your next thought is, that is your message from your loved one. Trust it. You don't need validation from anyone else. Let your soul express it-self and speak to you. Let your subconscious mind speak to your linear mind. Don't let your conscious mind analyze it too much!

There were times when I was writing that I listened to my intuition and not to other people. I would receive advice, think about it and stay strong in my belief for some things in my book. I remember thinking about the part in the book where I write, "**I guess having four children to deal with, there wasn't much time to help me deal with my insecurities, or other such silly things, like not making the softball team.**" **~Monica L. Morrissey** For some reason, I felt that this particular memory was important. I didn't explain it anymore but I knew that it had to be included. The reason it needed to be included would come almost a year after my book was published.

I am now an instructor for Southern New Hampshire University. I teach Master's classes to teachers in the same program that I received my Master's degree. A few weeks before the Spring 2020 class begins, I start finding feathers all over my house. I know that some people believe this is a sign from a loved one in Heaven. I have no idea who would be sending me feathers. I've never had so many feathers!

I receive the roster for a new class starting and I notice a familiar name. It is the name of one of my softball coaches; the coach who helped make the decision that I would not make the team. I immediately remember that part in my book.

During the first class, I share a lot about my career path and how I have grown as a person. Jean shakes her head as I share how sensitive and shy I was as a child. I explain that curriculum is important in education but so is the relationship between the teacher and the student. Every child deserves love and each child is more than a test score. As I share, I begin to pick up on an energy in the room. One that goes beyond our five senses.

Jean laughs about how much difficulty she has with technology. All of the students receive the email I sent to them. Jean's is lost in the cyber world of technology. She grins as she tells stories about her first graders going down the hall to get help from the IT department. She says that the same is true for her husband. They have difficulties with electronics at home too. I ask her if she understands that this might be a sign from

Heaven. She says that she has never heard of that before. *She then shares that her daughter usually sends her feathers.*

*I realize the energy in the room is her daughter, who transitioned to Spirit too early in life. Her daughter is laughing at her Mom. She thinks the funniest part of the whole thing is that her Mom doesn't realize it is her daughter playing with the electronics. Now I understand why I needed to include the part of not making the softball team and I understand where the feathers were coming from. It was because Jean and I were meant to connect in a very different way than I would have ever imagined. On the outside, I would be her instructor during her Master's program. But, on the inside, I knew that I was here to help connect her with her daughter in Heaven; the universe had a plan all along.*

*I'm home from Florida and it's Sunday. I have been writing since I woke - stopping for a short break. My husband goes for a hike up a mountain. I found a dime on Thursday. It was in the sand, exactly on the path I was walking to go back into the condo. Now, as I write, my husband sends me a video. He was on top of Mount Pisgah and in the video he says, "I'm on top of Mount Pisgah and you'll never believe what I just found.....a dime. A Canadian dime but a dime no less." I crumble just like I did when the minister on the mountain asked if I have faith. The dime story will never be done. The dimes will continue on and on forever. I wonder why Dad sent a dime from Canada?*

### The End or The Beginning?

I thought when I finished writing, I was done. I didn't realize the work was just beginning. My brain knew what to do but I didn't feel it in my heart - my "other" brain. I hadn't felt it inside. The information I was reading about over the years was only knowledge, not yet born to internal guidance.

For my whole life I had followed the path "that had been stomped on by shoes." It was the place I felt safe. I followed the crowd by going to college and then having a career in teaching. Writing is taking me on a whole new shiny path. One where I needed to discover for myself where it might lead. *Is a new path in life calling you?*

### Questions to Ponder:

- What social media platform feels best to you? Twitter? Facebook? Instagram?
- What will be important information to put on your website?
- Where will your book be located? Online? Book stores?
- How will you get your book out into the world?
- What can you do yourself and what will you need help with? Ex. creating a website, accounting information, photos, etc.
- How are you accepting advice and/or criticism? Are you using the information to help you grow?
- What will your book launch entail? Where, When, Who, and What? Make sure to market it so lots of people come!

**"This book demanded vulnerability and raw honesty in a way I hadn't expected and frankly, I wasn't so sure I wanted to comply, at least not publicly. But I quickly realized that I couldn't ask you to do the brave, messy inner work of transformative change and opt out myself." ~Seane Corn**

**My Self Publishing Journey**
**Audio book**

I remember the day that I first started taping my audiobook. I had tried to do it myself based on the Do-it-Yourself information at https://www.acx.com/. I sent my audio recordings to the Amazon and they reported the files were not good enough. I didn't understand all of the language around sound bits, etc. I think about who I would be able to ask to record my audiobook. The answer came from an unexpected source. A guy that I went to high school messages me on Facebook. He is looking for a copy of my book. He decides to go to the local bookstore in town. He sends me a message that our Grandfathers used to be friends. I had no idea! He said he has pictures of our Grandfathers at the family camp. It dawns on me that Corey has created musical recordings. I ask him if he knows the name of anyone who might help me record my book. He did! Corey was brought to me right at the moment when I needed to be willing to ask for help. Thank you Corey! Colin McCaffery did an amazing job! (http://www.colinmccaffrey.com/)

On the day of my first appointment, I received a text from my son and daughter-in-law. They are on their way to the hospital to have their first child. *Should I cancel my appointment? Should I go to the hospital? Such a difficult decision!* I wanted to get my audiobook tape completed. I had so many people waiting for the audio version! I decided to go to my appointment and stop to text my son every so often. *Can you believe that as I was reading about souls and lessons here on earth, we were welcoming our first grandchild into the world? Only divine intervention can control such a synchronicity.*

Audiobooks cost a lot due to the time it takes to create them. I negotiated with my publishing company because I wanted to be the one to read my book. I didn't want to hire a professional reader - which costs even more money! I felt strongly that this was my story and my readers wanted to hear me read it. I purchased a package through Balboa where I would send the recordings to them and they would do all of the final edits to then put the audio version on a few different platforms. The whole process from start to finish took about seven months.

By this point in my writing journey, I realized that I was taking a leap of faith in everything I was doing. Just like my life as a Realtor, I had to know inside that this journey my book was taking me on was more about helping the world be a better place to live. I turned my ring around and welcomed every new experience and was happy when I thought, "Come What May."

**Book Signings**

I did several local book signings at local craft shows. I also sold my books at The Beyond Center Expo and Messages From Heaven, a local event. (https://www.thebeyondcenter.com/) I donated books for charities.

My Publisher offered a book signing opportunity in Toronto. It was going to cost me a lot of money, but it might help get my book get some attention in the Canadian market. I decided to do it and was so thankful that I did! Right before the event, I targeted the Toronto area with a Facebook Advertisement. Balboa Press refers clients to Authors Press (a Marketing agency) and this is the company I would work with. For one hour, I would give books away (this is why it cost so much - I personally bought all of the books!) and sign them for all of the readers who were there. It was amazing connecting with people. Some people would look at the title and turn away. When they looked back at me, they were crying. I heard all kinds of stories from people. "My Mother always sends me dimes." "My Uncle sends me dimes." My story validated for them what they always felt in their heart. While others were interested in the dimes, some were interested in the information about being an empath. I was helping them and it felt wonderful to share my story.

On the way home from Toronto, I phoned Merrilee (she is a very good friend of mine who helped care for my Dad). She said - "I can't wait to tell you a dime story!" She explained that she was getting out of her car and she found a dime. It wasn't a regular dime. It was a **Canadian** dime! She knew I was in Canada this very weekend! She couldn't believe it! *I wonder about the other Canadian dime that my husband had found on the mountain. Was my Dad trying to send me a message that the Toronto book signing was a good choice?*

**Blog/MailChimp**

At all of my in person signings and on Facebook, I collected emails. I used Mailchimp to be able to send out letters and my blog. I published my blog on my website, Facebook and Instagram accounts. People didn't always purchase my book at the event, but my story made them curious. When I sent out a follow up letter after an event or sent my blog in an email or Facebook, it reminded them and they might purchase the book.

I didn't think at first that I wanted to write a blog. I changed my mind as time went on. I wrote about one blog post a month and hope to be able to write more soon. I encourage you to begin this as well. I published them on Facebook and people enjoyed the short articles and updates about my second book and my audio book. It was a great way to connect with my readers.

## Chapter Eleven: 180 or 360?

"It's only in looking back that the dots begin to connect." ~ Steve Jobs

"If there are aspects of yourself you can't accept, it'll be near impossible to accept the same qualities in others. By learning to love fully your own humanity and journey- seeing it all as holy- you can learn to connect, in love, with the souls around you." ~ Seane Corn

I recently read Gabby Berstein's book, *Judgment Detox*. I realized how much time I spent judging other people. Constantly. Like all day long! I wanted to step away from this part of me. It was hard. One day I was about to tell someone, "You are so impatient!" I didn't. I thought about it but realized that anything that the universe is giving me is a reflection of what needs to be healed within myself; a lesson my soul needs to learn. I asked myself, "Where in my life am I being impatient?" In my book, Dimes From Heaven, I call this "Boomerang advice". The advice that I give to others is actually the advice I need to listen to! Anytime I have advice or a feeling about someone else, it is a time to look within myself and heal that part of me.

"In fact, being truthful feels lighter, freer, and, in the end, more liberating." ~ Seane Corn

Here is my story about being impatient:

I was training to be a Health and Life Coach. I was terrified to share this with people because I wasn't sure what people would think.

I posted an opportunity on Facebook as I needed two people to be my first clients to help me complete my certification. I posted it and got a little interest. One person committed, but I needed two. I waited a day and kept thinking that I either needed to post again or re-post my original post. I was most definitely worrying about what others were thinking and wondering how I was going to get another client. Within minutes of healing the impatient part of myself - facing it head on and admitting that I don't like waiting, someone messaged me asking about my post. The universe was sending me a positive experience when I was able to look within myself at my own judgments and took the time to reevaluate myself instead of pointing the finger toward someone else. The secret portal opening up.

It seems like the universe is like one big scavenger hunt. The universe leaves clues and if we are paying attention, we can follow them like bread crumbs. Sometimes it takes time to see how the clues fit together but looking back I can see now the signs supporting me were there along the way.

**"The first step is to remember that this kind of self-awareness requires no makeovers or do-overs; instead, it pulls back the veil of doubt, anxiety, insecurity, fear, blame, and shame, and reveals our true nature- which is basic goodness and, of course, love." ~ Seane Corn**

Now, when I am trying to understand life, I use the $180^0$ or $360^0$ rule. If I come upon energy that feels good, I go forward toward this experience. Like a line - $180^0$. If I come upon something that doesn't feel good, I turn around my thoughts back onto myself. Like a circle - $360^0$. I look within myself for the answers. When that happens, I need to heal the part inside myself that needs to be healed because every experience in life is here to teach me something. By listening to my gut, I know when to move forward or turn around and look inward. When I feel resistance, I know I need to go $360^0$ back to myself. Like a boomerang that, if thrown correctly, always comes back to you.

**"I had to run to a solution, not away from a problem, and I'm glad I did." ~ TJ Menhennitt from his book Taking the War out of the Warrior**

Gary Zukav and Linda Francis talk about the "earth school" in their book, The Heart of the Soul. They explain that we are all here to learn our lessons. In this earth school, it is important for us to turn inward (3600) to heal. If we don't the same lesson will be given to us over and over again. If I didn't face my fear and realize I was being impatient, more of those lessons would keep appearing in my life in different situations and different people. We need to look for patterns in our life - situations that are very similar. Jealousy? Anxiety? Fear? What is life trying to teach you? Use the 3600 rule to look within instead of complaining or judging other people or situations. The universe will support you more and more when you are willing to learn your life lessons. Otherwise, the same lessons will repeat over and over again until you learn how to solve them a different way. These lessons will be passed down from generation to generation until they are healed.

*If you began your career when you were young, do a 360⁰ turn-around and see what your heart is interested in doing. Maybe you might go in a different direction than you ever imagined!*

**Whatever you send out to the universe will be returned to you, just like a boomerang traveling back to its owner.**

**Here are some 360⁰ turn-arounds to think about:**

If you look at a plant and think it is a weed, do a 360$^0$ turn-around and look at it from a different perspective. Does the plant have a medicinal property that helps people heal? Well then, that "weed" is actually something to be grateful for. Why not call it a flower?

If you think you "see" what is happening in your life, do a 360$^0$ turn-around and be willing to look at the unseen forces in your life that brought you to where you are. Where can you find the universe working to support you?

If your conscious self is telling you one thing, do a 360$^0$ turn-around and be willing to examine your subconscious to see if your "programming" is actually controlling your thoughts. *What do you believe at a subconscious level that is controlling your thinking?*

If you feel disconnected in your life, do a 360$^0$ turn-around and look for places where you are able to connect. Maybe this is connecting with people, nature or God.

If your mind has been full, do a 360$^0$ turn-around and look for places where you can clear the clutter in your mind. This is where the magic happens and Spirit speaks to you. Take time to quiet your mind every single day. It will change your life. *I know it changed my life.*

If you are busy planning every single part of your life, do a 360$^0$ turn-around and try letting the day unfold without any planning. Ask the universe to help guide you. Then watch the miracles start appearing.

If you think things are happening "to you on the outside", do a 360$^0$ turn-around and look within yourself to see what needs to be healed within you. *What life lesson is the universe giving you?*

If you are uncomfortable, do a 360$^0$ turn-around and be willing to discover what might make you more comfortable. What's happening that is making you uncomfortable? Get curious about where this originates and be willing to let it go.

Just when you think something might be ending, do a 360$^0$ turn-around and realize that you are only beginning. Beginning a new life; free of thoughts and open to new possibilities.

Every opportunity in life that is given to you is an opportunity for you to learn.

In my first book, I spoke a lot about how our emotions affect our body. My father was a mechanic and he thought the doctors could fix his body just like a car. This is true for some things, but our emotions affect our bodies also. If we don't learn to face our emotions, our bodies will become ill. Medicine will only heal part of our illness. We will keep getting the illness back in our bodies if we aren't willing to face our emotions. These can be from long ago or more recently. Either way, it is important to move through them and release them. This is what will heal everyone. *Check out Louise Hay's book, You Can Heal Your Life to find the link between a physical ailment and an emotion. Hurt knee? Maybe you are going through a transition in your life.*

Changing ourselves is both difficult and scary, but it is also the only way to free ourselves from our own thinking. Our human brains have a built in alert system for signs of danger, especially anything that feels like a change to what we are used to; that which feels safe. The alert system is controlled by our Vagus nerve and it is responsible for our ability to fight, flight or freeze during an emergency situation. This nerve connects our brains to the rest of our body, controlling both the parasympathetic and sympathetic nervous system. It sends messages to and from our gut and to and from our hearts and other parts of our body. When we sense danger, the vagus nerve will tell the heart to pump faster; we won't be in control. Humans needed this nerve to find food, build shelter, be part of a tribe and basically stay alive.

Nowadays, the Vagus nerve is responding to every little thing; sensing danger when there actually is no danger. In Malik Chopra's book, Just Breathe, she explains that the fight, flight or freeze was made to run away from animals who were chasing us. She explains that kids are activating this nerve and the fight, flight or freeze response can come from a Science or Math problem or when they struggle learning how to read. In adults, this is activated by misread text messages or during meetings where someone says something that activates a past hurt within the person. *Where is your vagus nerve being activated in your life?*

**"This road led to a place my soul had been missing: Peace. It was exactly at that moment that everything was so clear that I knew the war had finally been taken out of the warrior." ~ TJ Menhennitt**

When I was writing, I turned toward the people who supported me and, when I came upon someone who didn't, I looked within myself for the answers. That was how my first book was written- from my soul. Looking inside is a long journey but it is so worth it. Learning how to shine our light brightly in the world will always be the true way to internal freedom. When I looked within to learn my life lesson, the universe was ready to support me.

**"Sharing your story is giving back to the world." ~ Christina Goetz**

Christina wrote a book called *Truth Be Told How to Overcome the Fear of Sharing your Truth and Unleash your True Potential from Within.* I want to encourage you to tell your truth. Write about it. Share with others. When we share our authentic selves, we feel connected. I hope this book has sparked something within you that needs to be shared.

**"When we heal the fractured parts of ourselves and learn to love who we are and the journey we've embarked upon, we will see that same tender humanity in all souls. This is the revolution of the soul." ~ Seane Corn**

I know now that everything is perfect within the Divine Timing. The door to the secret portal was open to me as soon as I started writing my first book. Writing has most definitely helped me heal from the inside. As humans, we don't always know the bigger picture of how everything works. It's like one gigantic puzzle piece and it is up to me to do my part. I want people to be healthy and feel a sense of belonging. Writing has given me the opportunity to share my story and begin a whole new career in life; something that I never dreamed would happen.

I continue to work on rewiring my brain and change the way I think. I am grateful for so many things in my life. I am grateful for the people I have connected with through my book and I am grateful for the opportunities that writing has given me. I am grateful for my family and wholesome food. I am grateful for understanding how important it is to appreciate every moment of my life. I am grateful that I feel the support from Spirit, God, My Angels and the Universe.

One of the ways that I worked to reprogram my brain is to write in a gratitude journal. There is a suggested abundance programming activity and I highly recommend it! For 40 days, write in a journal for 15 minutes everything you are grateful for. If you skip a day, you need to start again. It has to be 40 consecutive days and it has to be for at least 15 minutes. You'll be amazed at how your life will change! The thoughts will creep into your subconscious and all of a sudden you will be thankful for each small thing in your life. From paper clips to an apple - everything in life will be grand!

I am still wondering about this concept of subconscious vs conscious. In my first book, I shared the story about my father waking up from his nap, where he had quieted his mind, and said, "Hey- would it be possible to have those Liberty Head dimes from my collection made into a necklace?" *Did my father dream about necklaces? Was Spirit speaking through my father? Did he remember something from his childhood - something that he had seen but never talked about? Something that we would have no way of knowing or understanding at the time...*

**"The soul speaks in feelings, in longings, in yearnings, in deep knowing, in vibration, in signs, in nature, in people. It centers itself in the heart, and carries within it a blueprint for your life. You can't hear the calling of your soul if you don't create space in your day to listen to it." ~ Rebecca Campbell**

The reason I am wondering if someone sent him a message is because you will never, ever believe what I found the other day.

I had bought some toothpicks at the store. I hadn't planned to buy toothpicks. The universe led me to the toothpicks, which would then led me to something else. I went to the store looking for a lighter. When I went to the aisle where I thought they might be, I saw toothpicks. I knew that we were almost out of toothpicks so I bought some. When I returned home, I went to put the toothpicks into a special glass container that was from my father's house. The old toothpicks in there were broken so I decided I was going to chuck the old ones into the garbage. As I almost dumped the entire container, I realized there was something in the bottom. I reached in to grab it and this is what I found:

"Believe. Believe in Heaven. Believe in signs. Believe in the unknown. Believe in a bigger purpose. Believe in miracles. Believe that there is good in the world. Believe in yourself. Believe that I am always with you. Just Believe." ~ Monica L. Morrissey

# Resources and references:

1. Box, H., & Mocine-McQueen, J. (2019). *How your story sets you free*. San Francisco, CA: Chronicle Books.
2. Brown Brené. (2019). *Dare to lead: brave work, tough conversations, whole hearts*. Place of publication not identified: Random House Large Print Publishing.
3. Byrne, R. (2018). *The secret*. New York: Atria Books.
4. Campbell, R. (2016). *Light is the new black: a guide to answering your souls calling and working your light*. Carlsbad, CA: Hay House Inc.
5. Corn, S. (2019). *Revolution of the soul: awaken to love through raw truth, radical healing, and conscious action*. Boulder, CO: Sounds True, Inc.
6. Dyer, W. W. (2015). *I can see clearly now*. Carlsbad, CA: Hay House.
7. Gikandi, D. C., & Doyle, B. (2015). *A happy pocket full of money: infinite wealth and abundance in the here and now*. Charlottesville, VA: Hampton Roads.
8. Menhennitt, T. J. (2019). *Taking The War Out Of The Warrior: an inspirational journey through divorce & healing... into empowerment, self-discovery & spirituality*. S.l.: Balboa Press.
9. Morrissey, Monica L., (2019). *Dimes From Heaven: how coins and coincidences helped me discover my life as an empath*. S.l.: Balboa Press.
10. Northrup, C. (2012). *The wisdom of menopause: creating physical and emotional health during the change*. New York: Bantam Books.
11. Richardson, Cheryl. *The Art of Extreme Self-Care: 12 Practical and Inspiring Ways to Love Yourself More*. Hay House, Inc., 2019.
12. Runfola, Lisa Marie, (2019). *Limitless Life In A Powerless World*. S.l.: Balboa Press.
13. Scanlon, Maureen, (2019). *My Dog Is More Enlightened Than I Am*. S.l.: Outskirts Press.
14. Singer, M. A. (2013). *The untethered soul: the journey beyond yourself*. Oakland, CA: Noetic Books, Institute of Noetic Sciences, New Harbinger Publications, Inc.
15. https://www.quora.com/What-is-the-difference-between-conscious-and-subconscious-mind-in-simple-terms

16. https://www.elephantjournal.com/2019/07/what-if-all-i-want-is-a-simple-life-on-a-farm-amanda-whitworth/?fbclid=IwAR1ZNpUcDY1Kq_U1p_Vjvs68a7lWLN-_13IADhX7QEKUcJ4BTR6RWLHBcAQ

Monica lives in Northeastern Vermont with her husband. She has two sons and two grandsons. Monica taught elementary and middle school for twenty-seven years before changing careers to be a Curriculum Director. She never thought she would ever be a writer until the coins and coincidences kept happening over and over again. Now retired from education, she is a Master Reiki Practitioner, Inspirational Speaker, Past Life Regression Hypnotist, Health and Life Coach, and Intuitive Angel Card Reader. She enjoys helping people transform their lives.